Valley Writers

Monks, Miners and Moonshine
Northern history as it should have been

Bird sanctuary and tourist attraction, Marsden Rock has stood for centuries. But the arch through which boats could pass at high tide became unstable and in 1999 the decision was made to demolish it.

You're History

Sandra Salmon

The planning done, the wires laid.
The crowd is hushed, last checks are made.
A push. A pause.
A crack. A whump.
And Marsden rock is Marsden stump.

Valley Writers

Monks, Miners and Moonshine
Northern history as it should have been

Edited by Margaret Lewis

Drawings by Ron Gray and Sandra Salmon
Artwork by Betty Bone
Cover Design by Nicholas Leake

Published in Great Britain in 2000
by
Valley Writers
c/o 7 Hamilton Row
Waterhouses
Durham
DH7 9AU

Typeset and printed by Lintons Printers,
Beechburn Industrial Estate, Crook DL15 8LR

Valley Writers wish to thank
Durham City Arts and the Millennium Festival Awards For All
for their financial support.

ISBN: 0 9536034 1 5

This is copyright © Valley Writers 2000. All rights reserved. The copyright of individual contributors remains with the authors. The contributors have asserted their moral rights in accordance with the Copyright Designs and Patents Act 1988. No part of this book may be reproduced or transmitted in any form or by any means without written permission from the publisher, except by a reviewer who wishes to quote brief passages in connection with a review written for insertion in a magazine, newspaper or broadcast.

CONTENTS

                                                               Page

Frontispiece
You're History   Sandra Salmon

11th Century		
The King's Venture	Eve Stockmann	1
Is This the Place?	Sandra Salmon	6
The Building of Durham Cathedral	David Cummings	7
12th Century		
The Turning of the Screw	Eve Stockmann	11
13th Century		
What's Wrong with Autocracy?	John Gamblin	15
A Dragon in the Sky	Tina O'Neill	17
14th Century		
For Whom the Bells Toll	Eve Stockmann	19
Incident at Aldin Grange Bridge	Ron Gray	23
The Arrival	Alice Smith	30
15th Century		
Weekend Leave	John Gamblin	35
16th Century		
Payment in Kind	Sandra Salmon	43
Thou Shalt Want Ere I Want	Betty Bone	48
Purloined Progenitors	Sandra Salmon	55
17th Century		
The More Things Change the More They Stay the Same	John Gamblin	57
Scratching	Sandra Salmon	64
18th Century		
The Human Calculator	Eve Stockmann	65
Dress Optional	Betty Bone	69
The Hungry Sea	John Gamblin	76

Page

19th Century
The Ghost Piper	Sandra Salmon	81
The Train Now Standing	John Gamblin	82
The Vicar of Newburn	Eve Stockmann	87
A Man on a Horse	Tina O'Neill	94
The Nicky-Nack	David Cummings	100
The Price of Coal	Ron Gray	102

20th Century
The Greatest Showman	David Cummings	109
Thanks to Grandad	Sandra Salmon	115
Dorothy's Dream	Alice Smith	125
More Tea, Dad?	Tina O'Neill	130
Marshall Riley's Army	David Cummings	132
Uncle Albert and the DLI	Ron Gray	137
A Team of Experts	Betty Bone	144
Black Death	Janet Evans	151
Against the Odds	Janet Evans	152
The Jazz Band Outing	Tina O'Neill	153

21st Century
Aunty Mary and Uncle Bob	Toni Armstrong	155
My Nana Iris	Ryan Brown	156
My Grandma Grimwood	Sarah Grimwood	156
Christmas at 7 Albert Street	Sian Cruise	157
Memories	Daniel Thompson	158
Childhood Memories	Britonny Brown	158

Acknowledgements	160
Source Material	161

~ 11TH CENTURY ~

In 1072 William the Conqueror halted in Durham on his return from Scotland, where he had been fighting King Malcolm. Kingsgate owes its name to this episode, since this is where William made his hasty exit.

THE KING'S VENTURE
Eve Stockmann

'It's getting late, Sire!' Walter de Bensham had been instructed to lead the King's party to Durham and had planned to reach it while it was still light. The sooner they got to the commander's house the better. Just the other night two Normans had been murdered in Durham - presumably by locals - when they went out after dark and there was talk that the numbers of Normans killed under the cover of darkness grew at an alarming rate.

William halted his horse and looked at the scene before him. They had come to a clearing in the woods and the late evening sun was painting the trees in the distance and the meadow in front of them a mixture of gold and browns. There could not be many peaceful places like this left in the area. The peace will soon be shattered, William thought grimly, my soldiers will see to that. And they will go on laying land to waste until the people here accept that I am their ruler now.

He had to admit to himself that he, too, would resist being governed by a foreigner. But had he not, out of compassion - for which he cursed himself now - conceded many privileges to the English? He was sure that the inhabitants of Durham had benefited more than most. Did they thank him for it? Oh, no. Three years ago he had expected the local landholders to support him - after all they had been more than ready to make use of the privileges bestowed on them. Instead they encouraged the peasantry to arm themselves and to slaughter every single soldier of his 700 strong force. He had to send new troops straight away, of course, and, naturally enough, his soldiers felt vengeful and ravaged the area. William shrugged his shoulders; the people here had only themselves to blame for their current misfortunes. Let them eat horses, dogs and cats, he thought, it'll make them come to heel more quickly.

'How far to Durham?'

'About two hours.' Walter de Bensham knew the way well.

'Let's do it in less!'

With that William set the pace. The wind rushing past his face and the movement of the horse beneath him made him forget his tiredness. He knew that nobody would dare ride faster than him, but also that there was hardly anyone who could. Eventually he slowed down and turned to the Bishop of Bayeux, his half-brother.

'Not bad for an old man of forty-four, don't you think?'

'Not bad at all.'

'But?'

'But don't take it for granted, that you can ride at this pace the rest of the way.'

'You are not still worried about Saint Cuthbert?'

'Of course, I am. And so should you be. You were no less frightened than the rest of us, when he sent that dense fog and would not allow us to march past Northallerton.'

William laughed an uneasy laugh. 'So, where's the fog now, eh? No sign of it yet. Do we really know that it was Cuthbert who stopped our progress?'

'Hush, Sire, you must not speak like this. Do not insult the Saint, I beg you. You don't want to bring heaven's vengeance upon yourself, and maybe all of us.'

The King tried to make light of this. 'Don't upset yourself. Nothing happened last time we were here.'

'Probably because the monks had taken Cuthbert's body to Lindisfarne.'

'They may not have returned yet', William suggested hopefully. 'Bensham', he shouted across to Walter, 'do you know anything about this? Do you know if the monks are back in Durham?'

Walter crossed himself at the thought of the holy body being taken back and forth.

'I believe they are, Sire.'

'You see, Odo,' the King turned to the Bishop of Bayeux, 'Saint Cuthbert obviously doesn't mind us entering Durham, since he has hurled no spells at us.'

'He still might. Forgive me, Sire, but I do feel that you have to be cautious. After all, your troops plundered the cathedral on the last occasion. Even threw the crucifix from the high altar, robbing it of its gold and jewels. I know that you ordered the offenders to be delivered up to the ecclesiastics, but your name will be linked with this sacrilege for ever. That is why you have to fear the wrath of Saint Cuthbert.'

'I'm sure that I can appease him - and the Church.'

The Bishop of Bayeux raised his eye brows doubtfully, but stayed silent.

'I'll do it by nominating a new bishop to the See of Durham. I believe that there has been a lot of disquiet since the death of Egelwin twelve months ago?'

'There has been, indeed.'

'What do you say to Walcher as the new bishop?'

'An excellent choice, Sire. He is distinguished both by learning and by piety.'

'I'm pleased you share my opinion, Brother. Do you think that Saint Cuthbert will approve of him, too?'

'Sire ... !'

'I didn't mean to be disrespectful.'

They were now riding at a pace more pleasing to the Bishop of Bayeux and continued in silence. The King did not wish to be admonished any more about his lack of respect to someone who had died hundreds of years ago and whose remains were supposedly incorrupt. How long since anyone opened the coffin? Probably only the once, ten years after Cuthbert's death, and that was over three hundred years ago. The more William thought about it, the more he wanted to ascertain the incorrupt state of the Saint's body. Now was not the right time for such an undertaking. Maybe after he had made Walcher the new Bishop and also Earl of Northumberland. Surely such a show of generosity would impress the ecclesiastics and reduce the worries of his own advisers.

During the next few weeks William became increasingly obsessed with this idea and the longer he waited to speak to anyone about it, the more he was determined not to be deterred. As time went on he also grew more and more irritated by those who considered themselves to be of superior rank in the city. They were forever looking for ways to obstruct the building of the castle because they felt, he thought, that their influence might be reduced, once a more permanent Norman residence existed. That was true, of course. It was exactly because he wanted to impose stricter control, that he had ordered the castle to be built. At the same time it was going to be a fortress against the Scots, but the city elders did not seem to appreciate that at all.

One night, about a week after Walcher had been appointed Bishop of Durham, William could not contain himself any longer. The ecclesiastics had prepared a sumptuous meal for him, but the King barely noticed the food. He had made up his mind that he wanted to see the body of Saint Cuthbert tonight. As he announced his wish, hushed silence fell over the hall and everyone fell on their knees, crossing themselves feverishly. Walcher was the first to speak.

'Please, Sire,' he said, still on his knees, 'please do not ask this of us. To open the sepulchre of Saint Cuthbert would be sacrilege, and as an officer of the Church I cannot condone it.'

'I only want to see the Saint for myself. I want to see that his body is incorrupt.'

'It is incorrupt,' Walcher said forcefully.

'Have you seen that for yourself?'

'You know that I have not.'

'Has anyone?'

'No, not for some hundred years, but we do know that the body of the Saint is incorrupt.'

William looked at the Bishop of Bayeux who had his eyes firmly fixed to the ground and obviously did not want to be part of the argument. Then he saw two of the ecclesiastics putting their heads together and whispering. He could control his anger no longer.

'I do want you to open the coffin,' he said icily, emphasizing every word. 'In the event of his body not being in the state represented to me, I shall have all those of superior rank in the city, who dared to impose on me, put to death. This is because I have to assume that you deceived me.' William felt satisfied when he saw that these words caused great fear among those present.

'Open the sepulchre now!'

'We do have to send for a stone-mason, Sire.'

'Yes, yes, but hurry him up!'

Nobody spoke as they waited for the stone-mason to arrive.

Some of those present were numb with fear, others prayed quietly. Only the occasional dry cough or the almost inaudible swish of a gown broke the silence. Suddenly a gust of wind swept through the hall blowing all the torches out. Out of the dark a barely visible, almost transparent red cloud gyrated towards the King, enveloped him, lifted him from the ground and spun him round a few times. When he came to a halt he became aware of a stale, musty smell and could make out the faint outline of a figure towering over him who addressed him in a hollow drone.

'William the Bastard, you have committed sacrilege before and now you are about to commit the biggest sacrilege of all.'

The King wanted to defend himself and attempted to speak, but it was as if someone had put some burning embers down his throat and he could do no more than utter some grunts.

'You are not to kill any of those who believe in me', the voice droned on, 'but I shall put you to death unless you leave this city instantly, never to return.'

William felt so hot, he wanted to pull his clothes off. As soon as he loosened one garment he felt colder than ever before in his life. Then he was hot again. As the figure moved closer to him this sensation intensified. He felt his tongue swelling up and knew that soon he would not be able to breathe any more. While he was fighting for his breath the voice continued to drone, 'I shall put you to death, William.'

He had to make it to the door, to his horse. His legs gave way a few times, but he forced himself on. The door seemed to move further away with every shaky step he made. Never in his life had he felt so helpless and so lonely.

He stumbled out, tripped over, fell, barely managed to pick himself up again and all the time his head went thump, thump, thump. Finally he reached his horse and he dragged himself up somehow, fear of death giving him the strength he thought he could not muster any more.

He swore that he would never return to Durham, if only his faithful horse would carry him as far away as possible, and so he rode without stopping till he reached the Tees.

Malcolm III was present when William de St. Carileph laid the foundation stone of Durham Cathedral. Today, planning permission would have to be sought. No doubt objections would be raised about the difficulty of access and environmentalists would be concerned at the disturbance of wild life. Were things different in 1093?

IS THIS THE PLACE?
Sandra Salmon

'Do I understand, your Grace,
The Saint has found His resting place?
Forgive me, Lord, I disagree.
Come, look around you. Can't you see?
No, my Lord, I'm no soothsayer,
Only, Sir, a mere bricklayer.
You cannot dig. This solid rock
Will put your foundings all to...
And isn't that the river Wear?
Well take my word, it's much too near.
There's rising damp and creeping mould,
Gale force winds and freezing cold.
The whole of the design's at fault.
I do suggest you call a halt.
Can I help? I wish I could
But don't see how to make it good.
I'd like to help you build your Kirk
But, really, don't want part-time work,
And, truth to tell, I've heard men talk
Of a project due to start in York.'

On 11th August, 1093 the building of Durham Cathedral commenced. Bishop William de St. Carileph had the old Saxon Minster demolished, to make way for a magnificent new Norman Cathedral. The church buildings he had seen while exiled in Normandy inspired him. Together with King Malcolm of Scotland and Prior Tugot of Durham he laid the first foundation stones of the Cathedral. The story that follows is by no means a true one, as you will soon find out!

THE BUILDING OF DURHAM CATHEDRAL
(WELL MAYBE!)
David Cummings

Who would have thought, that I would be standing here today, trowel in hand, with these two fine examples of gentlemen, Prior Tugot of Durham, and King Malcolm of Scotland. It is a beautiful summer morning in August, and the year is 1093 A.D. We have just laid the first stones of what will be the most magnificent building ever built in the name of our Lord: Durham Cathedral. Mind you, it would have remained a dream, had it not been for that band of imbeciles that call themselves builders. *John Wayne and Son.* You can make of that what you will!

It all started about three months ago, on a mild February afternoon. I was relaxing in my lounge, goblet of wine in one hand, and recent tax records in the other, (one needs some kind of comfort when working out one's dismal financial state!) when it suddenly hit me: my home needed enlarging. The old Saxon Minster was too small, not to mention draughty. It definitely needed some improvements. So, I had the idea of a large extension to the side, and a smaller one to the rear — single story, of course. Can't increase the taxes too much to pay for it. The damn peasants would revolt. Another sleeping area, a bigger lounge, that's what I needed. I set about designing what I wanted immediately, and after two days of intense drawing (in between preaching the Lord's word, of course,) I had the finished plans. I had spent three years exiled, sorry, I should have said on holiday, in Normandy and I found the church buildings there to be wonderful. They possessed the most fantastic stone carvings which I had ever seen. Why not a little French influence on the back of this old, dilapidated building? Mind you, I didn't know if the new part would fit all right with the old building, it being made from wood and clay. Never mind, I thought, we'll cross that bridge when we come to it (as they will say in the twentieth century).

I only had to find someone to carry out the work. That's where Mr. Wayne came into it. I was told he was the finest builder and stonemason in the area. I wasn't told that he was the most stupid, brainless excuse for a human being that would ever walk this earth! I discussed the project with him.

'Not a problem, give me a few days to rustle up a couple of labourers, and my son and me will do the building work,' he said.

Oh dear God, how could I have been so stupid?

Day one was pretty much straight forward, taken up with the preparation work, mainly. Then, on the second day they arrived with large, heavy hammers. My plans were fixed to one of the kitchen walls, and the banging commenced. I realised pretty soon that I would have to leave, I couldn't stand the noise, the jokes and the breaking of wind, and especially the sight of those 'builders backsides' hanging over the tops of their leggings. It was enough to put one off one's lunch!

I had only been gone a couple of hours, discussing the finer points of the tax increases with Prior Tugot, when the door burst open. Standing in front of us was a small, weedy fellow, covered in dirt and caked mud, with a look on his face which told me that something bad had taken place.

'You, you must come quickly, Sire, something terrible has happened,' he spluttered.

'What is it?' I asked. 'What could possibly have happened to make you burst in here like this?'

'Please, you must come with me,' was all he could reply, as he opened the door and left.

I looked at my friend, the Prior, in amazement, and followed the little man out of the door. We rushed through crowds, and I realised that we were making our way back towards the Minster. That was when I recognised the peasant as one of Wayne's labourers. Now I was concerned, no, I tell a lie, I was very concerned! My mind was racing, wondering what could have gone wrong.

'I hope he has not knocked the doorway from the kitchen in the wrong place,' I said to him, sternly.

'No Sire, it's a little bit worse than that, I'm afraid,' he replied.

My heart began to beat faster as we approached the Minster. Henry, the labourer, hurried in front, then he stopped, looked at me, and pointed towards the Minster. Or where the Minster used to be. I was dumbstruck. It was now almost flattened. I ran to the ruins and stood, shaking my head, saying out loud, 'Why me, why me?'

Then I spotted him, Mr. Wayne, attempting to strengthen one of the few pieces left standing. My blood boiled, and the Devil must have taken over my body. I remember a high-pitched scream, my scream. With eyes bulging I ran at him and launched myself, my hands finding his throat. I don't know who was more shocked, him or me. As my hands tightened around his fat, sweaty neck, squeezing at his windpipe, I suddenly remembered that I was a man of God. I still hesitated, before I finally slackened my grip and let him loose. He fell at my feet, mumbling what I imagined to be an attempt at an apology.

'Get up! Get up you incompetent, grovelling excuse for a human. Get up and tell me what has happened here,' I bellowed.

Wayne scrambled to his feet and breathed very deeply inwards.

'And don't you dare leave anything out. I want to hear it all,' I said through gritted teeth.

Everyone stood still, as he commenced.

'We were just moving the block of wood from above the kitchen doorway, when everything fell. It all just collapsed, it was over in seconds, and there was nothing we could do. Not very good builders those Saxons, if you ask me,' he said.

'Well, I'm not asking you, am I?' I yelled.

'Before you say something you may regret,' he continued gingerly, rubbing his swollen larynx, 'I've had an idea.'

'I dread to think what it is, but come on, give us all the benefit of your wisdom,' I said.

'Instead of rebuilding the walls and repairing the roof, why don't we start from the beginning again, and build a new church. We can make it look like one of those French churches, you've told us so much about.'

'Cathedrals,' I corrected. 'They're called cathedrals, and if we are to do this, you will not be working unsupervised. I met a fine architect while I was staying in Normandy. I will summon him to come over and supervise the building work. That means he will be in charge of you!'

Wayne shrugged his shoulders and nodded in agreement. At least it had taken the heat out of his present situation. He gestured to his men and the clearing up continued.

And so, here we are today. We all rose from our beds early, to witness the commencement of building work on Durham Cathedral.

'Make sure your drawing materials are all prepared,' I said to the scribe as he found himself a good spot to sit and record the day's activities. Three seats had been put in place directly in front of where the first foundation stones for 'my' cathedral were to be laid. My French architect was busy screaming at Wayne and his motley band (under my instructions of course). Not understanding a word he said, they ignored him. He nodded towards me as my two guests of honour, Prior Tugot and King Malcolm of Scotland, and I took our seats.

Wayne junior carried the pail of grey, gooey mess which was to hold the first stone blocks in place, and poured it into position. Then his father, along with three of the labourers, struggled over, carrying one of the blocks between them. They were almost in position, when one of them let out a scream and the block slipped from their grasp, taking lots of flesh with it. The stone block fell to the ground, and Wayne and company quickly followed it. I suppressed the urge to laugh as I enquired, 'I do hope you are all all right?'

Wayne looked at me with pain all over his face and replied, 'Of course we are, Sire, just a little scratch.'

Luckily, for the occasion, the stone block fell to exactly the position which was required. This left only one final procedure to be carried out.

My two guests and I stepped over Wayne and one of his labourers, still crouched on the ground, though I am almost sure the Prior's toe punted Wayne in the groin area on his way. We all stood in position, smiling as the good scribe recorded the occasion. And that my friends, is how we came to lay the foundation stones of the magnificent building we call Durham Cathedral.

12th Century

In the 1140s, under the rule of Bishop William Cumyn, the Ursurper, scenes of utmost cruelty were a daily occurrence in Durham and its name became synonymous with 'hell upon earth'. His rule lasted for four years.

THE TURNING OF THE SCREW
Eve Stockmann

Thick smoke wove a grey ribbon round naked trees. They writhed their barren branches into a grey sky, like old women mourning the dead. Some houses were still smouldering, the occasional bright flicker dancing over charred beams. The inhabitants of Elvet had been trying in vain all night to save their homes and their belongings from the ravages of fire. They had been hiding when the soldiers, full of drink and the sense of their own power, came last night.

'Let's smoke the rats out!' With that the soldiers were setting fire to the houses and were splitting their sides laughing, when the people, who were desperate to avoid a brutal welcome, were driven out.

Roger Conyers and Bertram Bulmer could still hear the ring of their devilish laughter in their ears.

'These animals!' Roger spoke through gritted teeth. 'I wish ... No, it's no good to give in to fantasies. We have to work even harder to find more men willing to fight the Usurper. The men have been terrified of torture, but by now ... most want to die rather than suffer any more of this, I am sure.'

'Can there ever be an end to it?'

'This is not like you, Bertram. You never give in, you always ... '

'Yes, but seeing the place where you spent most of your life, in ashes ... And so many dead ... '

Roger's face hardened. 'I've been there, too. Believe me, I know how it feels. And now ... now I've got so much hatred in me, it sometimes feels as if it's going to suffocate me. I will not rest until we are released from William Cumyn's yoke.'

'Neither will I'. Bertram's voice was full of bitter resolve.

'The worst is, Bertram, I really trusted King Stephen and King David five years ago. I should have known better, but they were so convincing in their promises to make the peace treaty work.'

'I never trusted the Scots. And this David, his only interest is to enlarge his realm so that he has enough land to bestow on members of his - how do you say? - governing elite.'

'That's obviously not good enough for the likes of Cumyn,' Roger snorted.

'Exactly, that just proves my point: you can't trust the Scots. And he is a particularly loathsome example.'

Their thoughts went back four years, when Bishop Rufus died and when William Cumyn, the Scottish Chancellor, usurped the See of Durham, ignoring any attempt which had been made previously to improve relations between the Northumbrians and the Scots. He knew that most of the barons could be bribed easily enough and that they would help him gain control of the castle. The monks opposed him from the very beginning but it took two years, until a small band of them managed to outwit Cumyn's guards and got away to York where they elected a lawful bishop, William de St. Barbara.

Roger interrupted the silence with a sigh. 'Looking at this devastation I can almost understand those who blame us for supporting Bishop de St. Barbara.'

'Do they really believe that Cumyn would not have found another reason to torture so many people, irrespective of what we did? The man is a beast. And he is forever suspecting plots against him.'

'He is not so far wrong there.'

'True. I wish one would succeed and that he suffered all the pains of hell.'

'And eternal damnation!'

'Surely, after what he did to the monks ...'

'While they were at prayer ... '

'Yes, and after keeping the Cathedral closed to worshippers and pilgrims for over a year now ... '

' Eternal damnation is a certainty!' They said it together and at this moment imagined hell to look something like what stretched out before them. Picturing William Cumyn in it, threatened by hell fires, begging for mercy, filled them both with immense satisfaction.

Through the haze Roger made out the shape of a rider approaching and turning towards him he shouted, 'Galfrid, is that you? Are you bringing more bad news?'

'The Ursurper's nephew is gathering his men in Merrington.' Galfrid d'Escoland brought his horse to a halt and his eyes fell on a magpie feeding on a dead dog. His hands tightened round the reins.

'You would think they had done enough damage for some time,' Bertram scowled.

'No, it's not what you think. There is talk that he wants to turn the church into a castle.'

'Into a castle?' both, Roger and Bertram, echoed. They could barely grasp the enormity of what had just been said.

'Surely, even Cumyn and his nephew can't go as far as to profane God's altar. You must have misunderstood.'

'I tell you, William Cumyn wants to be rid of the church and wants a castle there, instead. A man who is capable of forging letters from Rome surely cares very little for God's will, or for the salvation of his soul.'

'We can not let Cumyn and his nephew profane God's altar!' Roger declared in a voice hoarse with hatred. 'He thinks that he has beaten us into submission, that we'll find it impossible to collect enough men to stand up to them. But we must! Every old man still able to walk, every young boy who can shoot an arrow, they all have to fight these damnable men who believe that they can put themselves above God. I rather want to die than allow that church to be made into a castle.'

A few weeks later the three barons moved their hastily collected force to St. John's in Merrington. The Usurper's nephew had been pressing his men hard to bring about the change from church to castle. They had almost completed a moat around the church and had just finished some new outworks. Since there had been no obvious opposition to the work so far, the Scots had diminished their guard.

At first sight of the motley squad, someone joked, 'Hey, look, the people of Durham want to invite us to one of their famous bonfires!' As they approached though, quietly but resolutely, the joking soon ceased. Some of Cumyn's men hurriedly barred themselves in the church, others manned the tower. All of them grabbed whatever weapon they could find but soon realised that their collection, which consisted largely of shovels and stones, was a poor match to the darts and arrows of their opponents.

Roger, Bertram and Galfrid led the charge against Cumyn's men. The hatred they all felt, the abhorrence of the evil they were facing here, gave them unknown strength. They forced their way through the church windows and hurled firebrands at the Scots, their arrows sailed up the tower and found their human targets with surprising accuracy. Many of those offenders attempting to flee, found themselves trapped in their newly dug moat. Every sign of victory was followed by the cry, 'Long live Bishop de St. Barbara!'

When Cumyn's men admitted defeat, the triumphant men went into the battered church to say thanks to God for saving St. John's. As they came out, Roger turned to Bertram, 'It looks as if there is an end in sight, after all!'

13TH CENTURY

The central tower of Durham Cathedral was started in 1233. In 1234 Newcastle suffered a plague which lasted for over three years. By 1238 the Burghers of Newcastle began to feel like a minority ethnic group and, never slow to further their interests, probably decided to protest their rights, with a letter to Ofking. The King's reply, in this imaginary exchange, granted a charter which accidentally started the Coal Trade from North East England.

WHAT'S WRONG WITH AUTOCRACY?
John Gamblin

January 1238
Sire,
 We think our town is being neglected. Today in Durham is being erected a tower, for which you gave permission, and ignored the same submission for our church which, as you know, and architect's reports will show, is standing in much worse condition. By deeming it less than propitious gave fullest reign to the superstitious, whose arguments, indeed, are vague - that a towerless church invites the plague. This fearsome plague, now three years old, demands your subjects make so bold, as to invoke Majesty gracious for succour swift and efficacious, to bring our town in from the cold.

December 1st 1239
Burghers of Newcastle,
 Your plague is in the past, I hear. From that we have no more to fear but regarding yours of '38; I've truly had much on my plate and find it difficult to relate to such minutiae of state, although, of course, as you should know, concern for the North moves really slow. But, to accuse me of neglect is something that I must reject and ask how much you men expect.

In '35 I granted you a liberty, given to very few, that in your walls, resides no Jew. And then again in '36, when Scottish Lords renewed their tricks, I was not slow to intercede with gold to satiate their greed, that whinging burghers would not bleed. Now, at great length, I'm told to bring your town in from the cold. Your town to the Scots, I should have sold, to rid me of pervasive mould.

Ah well. I'm not disposed to barter and to behead would only martyr, so by this Seal you have my Charter. Go outside your walls to moan and work your fingers to the bone by digging and removing stone. Then if, by chance, within that hole you happen on a lump of coal, hard labour never harmed the soul, if warmth is a most pressing goal.

In 1275, on St. Nicholas' Eve, a great earthquake was felt in Newcastle. There was dreadful thunder and lightning. A blazing star appeared and a comet, looking like a dragon. This terrified the people.

A DRAGON IN THE SKY
Tina O'Neill

Hey, Bill, come and look
There's a dragon in the sky.
Hey, Ma, did you see?
I think he winked at me.

Can you hear the roar?
Can you feel the shaking?
Ma, don't cry.
No one's going to die.

What can it mean?
Why should we hide?
It's a wonderful sight.
No need to fight.

The stars still shine.
The world's still here.
There's a dragon in the sky,
And no one knows why.

14TH CENTURY

In 1327 the Scottish army was raiding the country round the North Tyne Valley and reportedly also came to the Abbey of Blanchland, which nestled in the Derwent Valley, surrounded by steep slopes either side. It was almost cut off from the outside world. Blanchland, which means White Land, probably got its name from the Premonstratensian canons, or 'white canons', who lived here. Unlike other monastic orders, the Premonstatensians preached and worked in the parishes near their abbey.

FOR WHOM THE BELLS TOLL
Eve Stockmann

'What is it, Brother Giles?'

'I thought I heard something.'

The Abbot raised his dark brows in indignation, so that they almost met his white cap. 'If you would spend less time listening for things which are not there, but concentrated more on your records which are in a deplorable state, then - maybe - we would both be happier.'

'But, Father ...'

'No, Brother Giles, I don't want to hear any more of this. How many more times do I have to tell you that we are perfectly safe here? Can you not remember how difficult it was for you to find the Derwent Valley? Did you not tell us that you were tempted to give up looking for us, after wandering through the woods all day without a sign of the Abbey?'

'I did, but I could not find my way back either,' Giles muttered down to his white cloak. At this moment he would have loved nothing more than to be back on the farm again and not here in Blanchland, face to face with his Abbot who never seemed to be unsure of anything.

'That is exactly my point, Brother Giles: if you could not find the way, why should the Scots find it any easier?' With that the Abbot straightened himself to his full height and smoothed out his cloak in a manner which indicated that that had been his final word on the matter.

Giles knew that any further comment would earn him nothing but a lecture about the importance of constantly disciplining thoughts and emotions. However hard he tried, though, his thoughts and emotions refused to be disciplined at the best of times, leave alone now. A few weeks ago a Scottish army had been raiding the countryside nearby and King Edward III and his army had come to stay in Blanchland for one night, expecting to fight the Scots the next day. Giles could not forget the whispered tales of violence and torture he had heard during confession. Since then, when the candles were painting shadows over the cloister walls at night, he imagined Scottish soldiers stretching out long arms from behind the pillars, bearing weapons which promised certain death, and during the day even the sound of rustling leaves made him jump. True, the Scots had escaped back over the border that time. The other day though, on his monthly visit to Bywell St. Andrew's, people were talking again about the Scots being in the area and helping themselves freely to whatever they needed.

How could the Abbot not hear the rhythmic pounding of hooves, which was getting louder and louder, how could Brothers Jacob and Ambrose continue with their writing, as if nothing happened? Were they even more frightened of the Abbot than he was? Why did they not say anything? Why did nobody support him? The pounding of the hooves grew louder - or was it just the thumping of his heart?

'Horses!' Brother John's red face seemed even redder than usual when he burst in from the cloister. 'I can hear horses'.

He was followed by Brothers Benedict and Dominic who opened their mouths at regular intervals and probably said something but could not be heard because everybody had forgotten about the disciplined silence.

'We have to hide the treasures!'

'There's no time. We have to hide ourselves.'

'We should have listened to Brother Giles.'

'Quiet!' The Abbot's voice drowned all the others. Then he knelt down and started to pray, 'Our Father ... '

Giles mechanically uttered the words which he knew so well. But what if the heavenly Father could not help them? What if he never saw his own father again and could never put his arms round that old man's bony shoulders again? What if he could never tell him, you did right to send me to a monastery, I have come to accept it? What if he could never show him that he loved him? What ...?

' ... And peace be with you.' The Abbot had finished his prayers. It had become dark in the church. Everyone listened out for the sound of horses hooves and the clanking of armour.

'Can you hear them, Brother Dominic?' Brother Benedict had been getting increasingly deaf during the last year and as usual he turned to his friend for help, but he did not really expect to get a reply because all eyes were on the Abbot who was slowly moving towards the door.

'The Lord God will protect us.'

As they all followed the Abbot outside they were met by a thick blanket of mist which engulfed Blanchland. If Brother Benedict was moved by this miracle, he certainly did not show it, for his question came again, 'Can you hear them, Brother Dominic?'

The fog muffled the sound of voices demanding direction, of armour giving trees a brassy embrace, of subsequent curses.

'The Scots are still looking for us, Brother Benedict, but the Lord is helping us.' The Abbot had put his hand on the old monk's arm, as if to comfort him and Giles, for the first time, thought of him as a kind man and not only a disciplinarian.

'This is our chance to go and hide. Quick, follow me.'

The Abbot led the way, supporting Brother Benedict who was always in danger of tripping himself up with his cassock when he was upset. The others followed quietly, aware of the proximity of the Scots.

'Let's get down this here bank. We'll find the Abbey, I'm sure,' they heard someone shout. They followed the sound of horses hooves in their minds and shuddered at the thought of what so easily could have happened to them .

Suddenly they heard a horse neighing in terror, something skidding on slippery soil, branches scratching metal fast and then a thud.

'Poor animal.'

For a second Giles thought of the Scottish soldier as almost human but changed his mind immediately.

'I bet these cursed monks got God to help them.'

'And we have to help Him distributing their treasures amongst the needy.'

'Yeah, the needy - like ourselves,' someone chuckled.

'There's no point now. We can't afford to lose any more horses or men. This confounded fog could last for days and while it lasts we've got no chance of finding the Abbey. Much better to turn round now and to come back another time.'

Giles held his breath when he heard these words. It was wrong of me not to have trusted the Lord enough, he thought ruefully. How can I go and spread His word when I don't believe in it sufficiently myself? I was only thinking of myself when the Abbot and my brethren prayed for a miracle and yet, I, too, have been saved. We have seen proof of His power and love, and I will tell the whole world of this. I must. Now.

He left his hiding place and hurried to the church as quickly as he could. The echoes of the horses hooves, growing fainter in the distance, did not frighten him anymore. As he started to ring the church bells in praise of God, he felt as if he was being lifted to heaven. He wanted the whole world to hear of the miracle which had happened and as the sound of the bells was carried along the valley, he was happier than ever before in his life.

The Scots turned round when they heard the bells, found the Abbey and burnt it. They also found the Abbot and his canons and slaughtered them all.

In October 1346, after the battle of Neville's Cross, King David of Scotland failed to make good his getaway and was captured.

INCIDENT AT ALDIN GRANGE BRIDGE
Ron Gray

Prudence placed the cauldron in the middle of the fire. When it started to boil she tipped different kinds of vegetables into it. From a blood-splattered table she scraped together bits of meat and it, too, was put into the steaming, hissing vessel. She felt a tap on her hip. It was her young daughter, Meg.

'Mam, can I help?'

Prudence spun round, 'You might cut yourself. Away to the gate.'

'Aw, Mam.'

'Shush, little woman. Now, get yer sell to the gate and watch for them come'n. Thee might have a turnip for ya.'

She squealed with delight and ran to the gate overlooking the broad meadow. In the distance were two figures. Father and son were walking towards the little cottage. She stood to her full height and waved, but the two were engrossed in conversation.

'Ah tell ya, Da, it's not reet, we have to fight their bloody battles. Ah mean whadda thee iver dee for us? Taks them arl their time to tark to us, and when thee dee its arlways some sort of order!'

Tom, the father, shook his head, 'Billy, that's treason tark, lad, and ya knarr what thee dee with traitors! Now, ah knarr tho's started court'n an' iverything, but these things 'ave got to be done. If thee win thee'll level the countryside.'

'Aye, a suppose tho's reet. Ah couldn't stand't if owt happened to Charity. She's that delicate; she's like a little flower in the breeze, and she's that kind an' generous...'

'Son, ah dinna want to hurt thee feel'ns, but tho knarrs when thee say she's generous...'

'That's just tavern tark....Aye up, here's somebody come'n.'

A man on horesback approached them against the backdrop of the cathedral. He pulled the sweating animal to a halt in front of them.

'The camp fires 'ave been seen, so get ya gear together and be at Merrington the day after next, and nee arguments!'

The horse shied a little, and as it did Billy turned to his father.

'It's arl reet for him. It taks a battle for 'im to speak to the likes of us!'

The rider wheeled his horse round, 'What was that? Is he refuse'n to fight?'

Tom stepped in, 'The lad didn't mean nowt, me Lord. Ya knarr what young'ns are like nowadays. Arl gob!'

The rider tapped the hilt of his sword, 'In future, keep half thee mouth shut or ha'll githa a taste o' this!' - and with that he galloped away.

Billy couldn't resist a parting shot, 'Only mad 'im a knight cos' his Da got Hatfield the Bishop's job.'

They reached the tiny hovel where little Meg was swept up in her father's arms, 'Who was that man, Da? He looked clean. Is he one of them that wash every week?'

Prudence chastised her, 'Don't be silly, girl. Nobody washes every week. Now go and fetch the nettle soup for Billy and ya Da.'

'Ah hope ya haven't been pick'n it where the dog's been empty'n its bladder?' Billy said.

Both father and son grew silent. Prudence sensed that something was wrong, 'What did that man want? Was he sent by the landlord? The rent's not gann'n up again, is it?'

Tom stared into the fire, 'It was a squire, tell'n us to gan to Merrington.'

'Merrington? But that's miles away! Tell 'im ya not gann'n!'

Billy grabbed his father by the shoulders, 'She's right. Why should we risk our bloody necks just to keep the toffs dripp'n in gold and land. Our land! The Bishops are nee better, parade'n aboot the streets, tell'n iverybody that thee'll gan to hell if we dinna give them our last farth'ns. And what dis he spend it on? Lang silk dresses. He must have a cupboard full of them. Made in the Orient...'

Little Meg put her hand up, 'Is that the tailor's on the bridge?'

'No man! Ower the watter. The salty watter. And here's us, live'n like pigs in a pigsty without so much as a penny between us, and they want us to fight a battle for them!'

Mother threw her arms up, 'Battle? Oh God! So that's what he wanted. Ya right, son, ah'll load the cart up.'

Tom stood, 'Noo just a carrot-pick'n mark on the candle here! Who's the gaffer in this hovel?... That's reet; Tommy Boy! ... And ah say, if Teddy Three wants us to fight that big puff, King David, then that's exactly what we ganna dee! ... Now, woman, gan and sharpen me axe till tho can comb thee hair in it!'

Billy was undaunted. 'But what aboot if we come back in bits. Me mother and oor Meg'll starve to deeth!'

Prudence tried to ease the situation, 'But we arl ready starv'n, son.'

Billy shrugged his shoulders, 'Arl reet, ya've gorrus there. But what aboot me Da? Surely ya'll miss me Da?'

Mother seemed to be deep in thought and this was only broken by Tom's voice as he said, 'What ah ya think'n aboot, my beloved?'

Prudence stooped, then opened the oak chest, 'Ah'll sharpen ya axe, pet.'

'There see! Ya mother's a true pat,' Tom exclaimed.

They sat in silence and tore lumps from the rabbit's carcass. After a while father and son went for a walk, and, with other people, watched the camp fires of the Scots army on the hills of West Durham.

'Ah'll nivver see Charity again,' sighed Billy, 'That lovely smile...'

'Aye, she has a nice set of teeth. Ya mother had them once.'

'Dad?'

'Aye, son?'

'Why do thee wear them kilt things.'

'Why should tho ask that, lad?'

'Ah mean, thee look like women,'

'Dinna be daft, lad, thee just idle fond.'

'How come?'

'Cos it macks it easier for them when thee gan to the bog.'

Although Billy constantly argued with his father, he had to succumb to his father's words of wisdom.

Prudence and little Meg were already asleep when they returned to the hovel. Tom and his son joined them on the straw. Tom noticed two rats playing 'wheel barrows' by the light of the oil lamp, 'Look at them two; not a care in the world. If a iver come back on earth, ah want'a be one of them.'

The oil lamp flickered, then died.

The next morning, the October sun tried to break through the dismal clouds as Prudence woke. Her thoughts were of the local muckspreader a couple of fields away, who lived in a converted pigsty. He was a bachelor, due to his occupation, but as Prudence had lost her sense of smell long ago, she reckoned he would still be a good catch - that's if the unthinkable happened.

Tom snored loudly, making her feel guilty, so she rose, brushing the cockroaches off her rags before preparing breakfast. As she did, she pondered over the possibility of losing her husband and son. Her thoughts were broken by Billy shouting from the netty at the bottom of the garden. 'Will somebody fetch some dock leaves?'

A crowd of men walked by. They, too, had been called to arms.

After a tearful farewell, Billy and his father were marching with them and singing battle hymns, omitting swear words as they were accompanied by monks. Billy was given a pike by one of the sergeants with a warning, 'Mind if tho damages that tho'll have it to pay for.'

'But what if ah get me heed lopped off?'

'The army thinks of iverything, lad; ya bones'll be boiled down for glue.'

'Just ask'n.'

After joining the rest of the English army at Merrington, they set off towards Durham, with hearts in their mouths at the thought of meeting the superior force of wild Scotsmen. They marched on between the rivers Deerness and Browney on their right flank and the river Wear on their left. Tom and Billy were in Lord Percy's division.

As they neared the Scots, they heard the beating of shields, and when in earshot both sides traded insults.

'It's a good job we dinna knarr what thee shout'n,' Billy said.

'A dinna think it'll be an invitation to a barn dance,' Tom answered.

'Why 'as a lot of them got ginger hair, Dad?'

'Cos thee Celts.'

'Celts?'

'Ah think it's some sort of swear word, lad.'

A mounted knight from behind leaned forward in his saddle, 'As ye han herd, herkaneth what that I shal seye: Jesus Christ shal bring thee forth.'

Father and son looked at each other, puzzled. Tom bowed to the knight, 'Good knight, we are of lowly birth and nee better than dog turds and nivver mix with the likes of thee sell. What ah'm try'n to tell tho is, that we haven't a bloody clue what tho's on aboot.'

The knight leaned forward and looked round, whispering, 'We've got to tark like this 'cos it separates us from the scum. To tell the truth, ah hate being a knight, but iver since thee promoted me Da to chief executioner in Durham Prison, he insisted on me takk'n the vows. Arl that push'n people aboot, collect'n taxes, putt'n people out 'o' their hooses, nor, it's not for me.'

Tom looked over to their left. Rows upon rows of archers raised their bows skywards, the newly honed tips of their arrows glinted in the October sun. The deafening roar of the Scots died as they watched the bowmen move as one. A faint cry of, 'Loose!' and four thousand yew bows tried to straighten. Like deadly rain the heavy ash arrows thudded into horses, the bodies of men, crude wooden shields and anything else that lay in their path. Pandemonium replaced the taunting. Horses panicked, bucked, throwing riders on to the freshly bloodied earth. Another storm, high into the blue sky. The English could hear a noise like someone throwing nails onto a metal sheet as arrows rattled off armour.

Before the archers drew again, the Scots who were still able, ran headlong into the English axes, aloft. The High Steward rode among the screaming, hacking men, their bare legs already drenched with warm blood of Englishmen. The archers fell back under the sheer weight of the Scots. The heart of the fighting came nearer to Tom and Billy. The knight's horse reared at the smell of blood.

Wounded men, holding their intestines, collapsed through the massive haemorrhaging of vital fluids. Their brains littered the ground.

The three braced themselves against the main body of massed tartan. Tom held his son, 'Let's show the bastards how to die, son!'

'Ah'd rather show the buggers how to run,' Billy said under his breath.

Just as the Scots were about to reach them, a charge of English cavalry thundered through, sometimes over the bodies of dead and dying. The Scots broke and ran, with the riders cutting and slashing at them.

The knight shouted through the din, 'Tom! Billy! Get a couple of stray hosses and come wi' me!'

They found some which were uninjured and followed the knight as he weaved in and out among the slaughtered. The carnage gave way to open fields. Groups of Scots on horseback and foot ran for their lives, some with the shafts of broken arrows sticking out of their bodies, leaving red footprints behind them.

Tom and Billy rode furiously to keep up with the knight and saw that he was in pursuit of a horse which stood out among the rest. It was adorned with the expensive trappings of royalty and its rider wore a suit of armour which shone with silver and gold adornments. The horse was obviously superior to theirs and it gradually pulled away from them.

After a while they lost sight of it and the three cantered forward, searching the hedgerows and gullies.

When he caught his breath, Billy asked the knight, 'Who are we supposed to be look'n for, Sir?'

'King David of Scotland.'

'Bloody hell!'

Tom followed a narrow stream which led to a small stone bridge about a hundred yards away. When he came to the bridge he called, 'Ower here. Quick!'

The knight and Billy rode to where Tom was staring at something under the bridge. It was the King's reflection in the water. An arrow was embedded in his shoulder, another in his thigh. They shouted for him to come out.

He stood, sword in hand, 'Ye'll have to kill me. Dee it fast with nay ceremony and away and collect yer honours. Ah trust ye'll have the grace to tell me yer names first.'

The knight dismounted and approached him, 'My name, Sire, is John Copeland, 'an there'll be nee mare kill'n today, so scabbard thee pigsticker.'

King David punched the knight with his gauntlet.

Tom grabbed the King and threw him to the ground, 'Kill'n ya want is it? Have ya not seen enough, ya bloody maniac? Thousands of men cut to ribbons back there and ya still haven't quenched ya thirst for blood. We work the bloody fields and break our backs for ya, and arl yea buggers dee is plan wars so ya can heap some mare bloody misery on us. Mare kill'n eh? It'll mak my day!'

Tom raised his axe above his head. King David of Scotland stood to his full height, 'I only ask yea to tell them that I died like a king.'

John Copeland stood between them, 'Put thee axe away, Tom. Dinna dirty thee sell with this scum. And besides, he'll fetch a canny bit ransom. Haway, Billy, tie him and bring his horse.'

They took him back, through the bloodied fields, littered with fifteen thousand Scottish dead. Dogs licked the blood off the grass. Women searched for their men among the grey, lifeless faces. The monks, who had been watching the battle from the cathedral, went back to their writing. Now they had plenty of material. It was over.

In the week to come there would be many funerals to attend. Later on they would erect a cross and people would pass it every day to remind them of the slaughter, yet madmen would still wage war and the people would mourn over their glorious dead. The cross would weather and break in half. No one will give it a second glance.

This story touches on the few days when the battle of Neville's Cross was being fought in October 1346. It is the story of a woman courageously coping with her fear as the slaughter erupts nearby.

THE ARRIVAL
Alice Smith

The day had begun well for Katrina. The dawn had brought with it the promise of radiance, the autumn nip soon to be dispelled by the warmth of the sun just beginning to nudge its way gently over the hill into a sky already showing signs of an azure blue. The house was contentedly silent, as she busied herself quietly about the kitchen preparing her breakfast, feeling grateful for the gift of these first few precious moments of peace, before the demands of the day ahead clamoured for her attention.

As she stood by the fire, stirring the porridge, she turned her head and let her gaze rest on the loveliness that lay beyond the window. Summer was over. The blaze of the flaming oranges, reds and russets burst upon her with such ferocity that for an instant she felt faint from the physical pain which shot through her as she absorbed the immensity of the beauty that lay before her.

Nothing of the events of the past few days, could be seen to have done anything to erase the familiar landscape, and it seemed that not even a blade of grass had need to send up its perfume of forgiveness. Was it just three days since her tranquil world had been shattered by the heart-stopping sounds of battle? Out of sight of the house, but within hearing distance, the clashing of shields, the whining of arrows, the meeting and thrust of spears, the thudding hooves of horses carrying English against Scot, Scot against the English, had filled the air. The screaming of horses and riders, as they fell to the ground in the agony of their dying, had stupified her into a state of profound and trance-like terror. Mesmerised, she had shut herself behind the door of her bedroom, unable to focus on the simplest of tasks, until the pangs of hunger had motivated her to make her trembling way down to the kitchen, to take a little of the soup, simmering in the iron kettle suspended from the hook over the fire, which Katrina in odd moments had remembered to tend. Automated by neccessity, urged by the pitiful noises coming from the barn, she had chanced leaving the house each day to relieve the two cows of their discomfort and feed them, at the same time giving some attention to her horse, Viking.

Often she would go to a window and look out anxiously for the couple, who for years had come daily to assist her with the running of the house and the farm, John and Helen, faithful friends, who would never willingly desert her, but for whom, for almost a week, she had waited in vain. Afraid and as puzzled as she felt, she was unable to find the will to leave the security of her home, even though that was, under the present circumstances, questionable.

Marriage to Jacob Belling, had brought her nothing but a life of unbearable loneliness for fifteen years. As a soldier, his tenacious loyalty to his King and regiment had surpassed all else, even the welfare of the wife to whom he believed himself to be devoted. Fervent in his love for adventure, the war with France was proving a solace for his soul, his existence occasionally confirmed by the odd messages reaching Katrina, delivered by the hand of anyone from France conveniently passing her way. Distance and time and the uncertainty of his return, had drawn a veil over much that they had ever known together and as there had been no children, there seemed little to nurture and prosper the marriage. There were days when Jacob scarcely entered her thoughts and when her concentration centred only on the ritual of keeping herself alive, never more so than now, when, at any moment, the enemy would be at the door.

Now, three days after the start of the fighting, all was quiet. Still ignorant of the circumstances and outcome, she had awakened this morning to a world strangely and wonderously silent. She had lain spreadeagled beneath the sheet, slowly becoming conscious of the stillness and a bright day filling the room. Rising, she had slipped out of her nightgown and hurriedly dressed in the clothes she had left ready the night before. And now she was feeling the welcome comfort of the warm fire she had stoked into life when she had come into the kitchen. She removed the porridge from the iron kettle and placed it on the table, but felt in no hurry to eat.

She walked over to the small window by the door, and scanned as much of the landscape which the scope of her vision allowed. She saw nothing to explain the sudden cessation of the horror which had terrorised her for the past three days. Even though as yet there had been no word of John and Helen, she happily hugged herself, and smiled as she caught sight of a lark rising from the meadow into the sweet clean air of the azure sky. Straight up and up it rose, its lovely song trilling back, mocking the earth-born weights from which it was now ecstatically freed. Her heart leapt, her own joy of freedom bound up with that of the bird, her own song harmonising with its song, and now as she followed it in its upward flight, she was carried deliriously into its company, and felt the sweep of its wings brush her cheek.

Katrina laughed out loud at the incongruity of her imaginings, but it bore out the lightness of her mood, which had been with her since she had opened her eyes that morning, and had first become aware of the wondrous silence.

Still at the window, she realised that someone was approaching the house from the path skirting the meadow and recognised Brother Jonathan. He was leading an oxen pulling a somewhat rickety cart. Reaching for a shawl lying on the bench by the fire, she picked it up, threw it over her shoulders and went out to greet her visitor, her smile reflecting the pleasure she was feeling.

She had known Brother Jonathan for most of her life. As children they had found in each other a shared love of the wild life contained in the woods and countryside into which they had been born. As they grew up, they had spent many hours together in an almost silent companionship, stealthily observing the nature shaping their young world. There were the times, when the young deer came nuzzling their elegant and graceful mothers. When the wily foxes ventured close to the farm, looking for food, they were lovingly coaxed to come and eat from their hands. Sneaking from their homes when darkness fell, they knew where to find the badgers, and would watch with great delight, as the lovely creatures playfully frolicked near the sett, blissfully unaware of their audience. They learned the names of the wild flowers and plants, growing in abundance at their feet. These innocent pursuits, bound them forever in a private and secret world of understanding. They were also part of a culture where the inhabitants of their village looked out for each other, giving them the freedom to roam unafraid in the woods and fields and the river which surrounded their homes.

The oxen came to a standstill at the door, and Katrina moved across to nuzzle her face against the animal's nose. She was surprised when Jonathan roughly grabbed her arm and steered her towards the house, to stand in the open door. There was anxiety and urgency in the tone of his voice when he asked, 'John and Helen — are they with you?'

'Why, no. I've not seen them — not in five days. Why do you ask?'

'Katrina, listen! Do you know what has been happening?'

'Yes, a battle. But I've seen no one — not until you have suddenly appeared.' Then seeing a pile of sacks on the cart she asked, 'You've brought the cart. Are you needing wood?'

Shaking his head, Jonathan took her by the hand. 'No, no wood.'

An expression of bafflement on her face, Katrina let her hand rest in his. Jonathan nodded towards the cart. 'Katrina,' and it was almost a whisper, 'Katrina,' he repeated, 'under those sacks lies a very badly wounded soldier.' He paused, for what seemed a very long time, wanting to allow her space in which to recover herself.

'He is a Scot,' he told her, 'the enemy!'

As he anticipated, Katrina was shaken but, without questioning, she walked over to the cart. Gently raising the sacks she gazed at the man laying beneath them. His grey eyes were open and filled with pain.

'Can we care for him?' Jonathan asked.

Katrina, recognising in a moment of self-knowledge that her world was about to change, turned to her friend and asked gently, 'Who is my enemy, Jonathan?

15TH CENTURY

In 1486, Monks at Rainton in Durham County learned how to mine coal from beneath the natural water drainage level. This is a speculation on how they might have developed the technique.

WEEKEND LEAVE
John Gamblin

 Brother Ullrick groaned in exasperation as he sat against the undressed stone in the corner of his minute cell. The only furniture, a wooden cot with its single roughly woven blanket, was forbidden territory until after Vespers and Ullrick was not tempted to add to the trouble already heading his way over the matter of the socks.
 A soft tap on his cell door interrupted his melancholy and the cautious opening revealed the face of Brother William, the dull light making his red hair appear even redder.
 'I saw the light under your door. Why aren't you at work?'
 'Why aren't you?' replied Ullrick.
 'I've been suspended.'
 Ullrick felt no surprise at the news. He had warned his friend often enough that his apprenticeship in the Abbey Brewhouse could be jeopardised if he continued to sample the production as liberally as was his custom.
 'What was it,' he asked, 'the ale or the mead?'
 'Hey, that's unfair! What makes you think it ...'
 'I've told you a dozen or more times that your addiction will earn you a spell of stable duty.'
 'My addiction? It's not "my addiction" when stock reaches its sell by date is it? Oh no. Then it's all, "Good Brother William." "Clever Brother William." "Do you need a hand, Brother William?"'
 Ullrick interrupted, 'OK. OK. Don't get your habit in a twist. It's your liver not mine.'
 'I'm supposed to test it, man. It's my job.'

'Your job is it? I know the Abbot says be happy in your job but I think he would see a difference between being happy and being merry,' retorted Ullrick.

William scowled irritably, 'What about you then?'

'I'm suspended, too.'

'Why?'

'Socks.'

'Socks? You mean those sheepskin tube things your mother made?'

'The same. Old Kendrick spotted me wearing them.'

'But he brought them in to you.'

'He did indeed.'

'Still, on second thoughts, I think you huffed him when you took the initials from the message on the package to give those things a name. "Sent Over Care of Kendrick, son". I mean, would anyone want to be connected with those raggy bits of lambswool? Socks! What a stupid word.'

'I don't know. He was all right until he stopped going to visit me Mam. That was after me Dad asked if he could learn to play the lyre too. Mind you, I could never understand how three of them would manage to play such an instrument in that one bed - it was crowded enough with only Kendrick and me Mam.'

'Hey, Ully, forget it man, cheer up. You knew you weren't supposed to wear them at work. Persocka non grata as Brother Claudius might say in the Latin class.' William laughed.

'That's easy for you to say, working in the Brewhouse. Just try sitting and painting cherubs and ivy leaves around capital letters for eight hours with your feet on a stone floor.'

'Aye I can see that but remember, in here, we all have a cross to bear.' William paused, deep in thought, 'I'm still puzzled. How did old Nosy spot them?'

Ullrick, head down, examined the stone slabs covering his cell floor with scrupulous attention.

'Come on,' William persisted. 'You always wear your habit long enough to sweep the cloister floor. How did Nosy manage to see your covered feet?'

Ullrick fidgeted. William waited.

William slapped his companion's tonsure, 'Hey, wake up man!'

'Lay off! That's enough. I was watching Sister Beatrice going to the Abbot's rooms.'

'Well, by my sanctified still! Watching Sister Beatrice were you? You'll end up in the stocks m' lad.'

Ullrick continued his appraisal of the stone flagging.

'And that begs another question', William continued, 'how could you manage to see her?'

'Through the window, stupid.'

'Not so much of the stupid, if you don't mind. That window is more than six feet high.'

'I stood on a chair.'

'You stood on a chair?' William emphasised each word.

'That's how Kendrick saw the socks.'

By now, socks had ceased to interest William.

'Let me get this right. You stood on a chair to watch Sister Beatrice going to the Abbot's rooms. Is that what you're saying?'

Ullrick nodded, his foot tracing the line between two slabs.

'How did you know she would be there? I mean; at that point; at that time.'

'She goes every day - straight after Matins.'

'And you watch her every day, of course.'

'When old Nosy is otherwise engaged. She's different to the others somehow. Y' know, when she moves. The others kind of glide as if they were on rollers but she, well, she bounces. Yes, that's it. Every part of her bounces.'

William joined his friend in stone slab contemplation. 'I wonder what instruction the Abbot is giving her', he murmured.

Ullrick could not concentrate at Vespers and afterwards, a restless conscience rendered sleep elusive. He did realise his good fortune in having a place in the Monastery. He had even avoided the waiting list after asking Brother Kendrick if he could see the lyre his mother was learning to play. He remembered his Mother sitting up in the bed and asking Kendrick to do something about 'that boy'. The Monastery gave Ullrick both an education and a calling, a circumstance normally denied to the offspring of farm workers. Increasingly though, of late, the eight years to his thirty-first birthday, when he would no longer be a novice, stretched in an endless path littered with restrictions, like rocks to make passage difficult.

He had, once, voiced his misgivings to William who, after anxious glances all around, agreed. 'I know what you mean. Just two or three hours outside the walls would make all the difference.'

'Once in a while,' Ullrick added.

Before he slept Ullrick had the embryo of a plan.

'I'm going to do penance,' he informed William the following morning.

'How?'

'I'll volunteer for latrine duty.'

William's face paled and his throat constricted to contain his surging stomach.

'That is penance indeed,' he gasped.

'Nothing less will do.'

William scanned the face of his young friend, convinced that all sense had left him. 'Why?' he asked.

'Because nothing less will convince them of my sincerity.'

'Ha! Ha! Ha! This is William you're talking to y' know, so let's have less of this sincerity claptrap, eh?'

'Just testing. Look, Willy, it's the only work that goes near to the old coal pit.'

'That's nearly as bad as latrines,' snorted William, 'What do you want with a flooded hole in the ground?'

'That hole in the ground goes under the wall.'

'So?'

'So, all we have to do is dig upwards on the other side of the wall and we can have Saturday nights with the lads.'

William stared in disbelief.

'Once in a while', added Ullrick, belatedly pious.

'All we have to do? Where do you get "we" all of a sudden? You're raving, Ully! Completely, utterly, hideously, stone barking mad.'

'We can do it', insisted the potential lunatic.

'There's that we again. Listen, Ully, once and for all. One half of that "we" thinks it's not only mad, but impossible.'

'Why?'

'That you have to ask, shows that all your marbles have spilled. First. The old pit is flooded. Second. If you could breathe underwater, which you can't, how far would you have to dig to come up on the other side? Third. Do you think a hole in the ground on the other side of the wall would go unnoticed? Fourth. Two monks doing the town with the lads on a Saturday night would be as inconspicuous as a grizzly bear in the chicken house.'

'You're just being negative. Take one thing at a time.'

'OK. How long can you hold your breath?'

'We won't . . .'

'There's that "we" again.'

'. . . need to.'

'What? Not need to. How's that?'

'Because there won't be any water.'

William, tapping his temple with a crooked forefinger, gazed sorrowfully at his companion.

'There won't be any water. Right! Do you mind explaining this miracle? This water vanishing trick. Where is it going to go, pray tell.'

'Down the latrine channel, that's where.'

'Uhuh, I see. This is where the "we" comes in of course. I'm on to you, Brother Ullrick. I expect your "we" plan includes you filling the buckets and me carrying and emptying them. Well, it's not on. No. No. No. I fill and you carry.'

'Good man. You're right. We'll make a good team.'

William grinned triumphantly.

'Now', continued Ullrick, 'you go and find as much rope as you can and as many rags as the laundry can provide while I go and arrange things at the Tannery.'

'Rope? Rags? The Tannery?'

'Of course. What's better than leather for carrying water?'

'Try wood. We already have wooden buckets.'

'Not buckets, dimwit. A tube - like the one Mam made for my feet - only longer.'

'And the rope and the rags?'

'Trust me!'

When approached, Brother Kendrick made no attempt to dissuade the errant novice from his intended penance.

'Lost time will be added to the end of your apprenticeship, of course.'

'Yes, brother,' said Ullrick meekly.

'And, as junior calligrapher, you will have to prepare the paperwork.'

'Of course, brother.'

'In triplicate.'

'Naturally, brother.'

Five days later, the Abbot was startled when his copy was presented by Kendrick.

'Don't you think latrine duty is a bit extreme for such a minor offence? I mean, the boy was only improperly dressed.'

'He volunteered for it, to show sincerity in his penitence,' Kendrick simpered.

'Oh! Right. But I mean to say, latrines?'

'I have heard you yourself say, Father, that if God had not intended us to shovel shit He would not have presented us each with a bowel.'

'Quite so. Very well, latrines it is.'

In the meantime William was collecting rope and rags. For every strand of rope and every stitch of rag he offered two prayers. The first, in piety, was for forgiveness and the second, in a fervent hope for undetected crime.

'Now what?' he asked, as he delivered them to the friend he now referred to, in the privacy of his brain, as "The Maniac".

'Come and I'll show you.'

Ullrick led him to a bucket filled with water and placed into it one of his "socks" through which a short length of rope held a bundle of rags. Immersing the sock so that only the upper rim was clear of the water, he pulled on the rope and the rags, tight to the side of the sock, forced a tubeful of water out of the bucket.

'See?'

Ostentatiously, William sniffed. 'I think so, but I could concentrate better if you would stand further away and downwind a pace or two.'

'Never mind that. Once we get the tube in place we'll empty this pond in no time.'

They worked incessantly, building a frame to hold the wheel around which the rope pulling the bundles of rags through the leather tube, would run. A wooden trough fed the liberated water into the latrine trench. Ullrick controlled a sluice gate, brushed the channel and, from time to time, checked the water level in the pit.

Their endeavours did not go unnoticed. Remarks from the Ropemaker, casual comments from the Tannery, took root and thrived in the confined hothouse of the Monastery.

'What are those two youngsters up to?' asked the Abbot. 'They appear to be working hard but are they observing their devotions?'

'Yes, Father.'

'Young men need to find an outlet for their energy. Don't you agree?'

'Yes, Father.'

'I think we should leave the reins loose while, at the same time, keeping a careful eye. What do you say?'

'Yes, Father.'

And so it was. Sooner than anyone expected, the underground lake was empty.

'Whheee,' screamed Ullrick. A sound which did not escape the ears of the watchers and within minutes a wondering congregation had assembled. Soon the Abbot arrived and a corridor opened through the throng to allow him pride of place. He sauntered through with Sister Beatrice bouncing becomingly behind.

William, winding the wheel, felt trapped. The Abbot smiled at him.

'The pit is dry now, I hear,' he said, 'does that mean we can dig deeper to obtain coal for our fires?'

'I suppose that is possible, Father.'

'Won't that be a pleasure?' said the Abbot, smiling at Sister Beatrice, 'But why is there so much water in the latrine channel.'

'Brother Ullrick is in charge of that department, Father.'

At that moment Ullrick emerged from his search for the best site to position the weekend exit.

'Ullrick. I'm curious about all this water in the latrine.'

'No problem Father. I simply open this gate and the running water helps keep the channel clean.' The Abbot nodded approvingly.

'Perhaps one day we might all have latrines with running water.' ventured Kendrick

'Take care Kendrick,' warned the Abbot. 'You are treading close to heresy. Do you imagine that if God had not wanted us to enjoy our own effluvium he would have given us all a nose.'

'Beg pardon, Father. My mistake.'

As the Abbot was leaving he called to Ullrick and William.

'Walk with us a little. We wish to speak with you.'

Sister Beatrice walked between the Abbot and Ullrick, who was so aware of the large mound of soft tissue brushing his upper arm, that he could scarcely concentrate on the Abbot's words. 'You have both done well. Is there anything we can do to show our appreciation?'

Ullrick glanced at William who appeared to be studying the effect of the wind on the tree tops.

'Do you think a weekend pass could be permitted Father?' A spasm passed over the Abbot's face. 'Once in a while,' added Ullrick hurriedly.

'Why would you want to leave us for a weekend, Brother Ullrick?' said the Abbot, icicles forming on every syllable.

'Well Father, it seems to me that if our Lord had not wanted his message carried to the most needy of His beings, He would not have created Saturday nights.'

16th Century

In 1569, The Rising of the North failed to restore Catholicism and the Earl of Westmorland, Charles Neville of Raby, was one of 60 hanged in Durham City.

On 8th January 1570, Sir George Bowes wrote to Lord Sussex that he had 'taken great pains to instruct the neighbours of the families of executed fathers to take particular care of the children,' which was all very well for him but were all the families lucky enough to have philanthropic neighbours?

PAYMENT IN KIND
Sandra Salmon

'Mistress Dickson!' Ralph Carpenter's bulk shadowed the cottage. Days gone by she would have welcomed him into her home. There would have been shouts and laughter as he swung little Mary into the air, or play-wrestled with young John, feigning early submission so that he could sit with a jug of ale and talk with Will — outside if the weather was mild or, should the day be inclement, in front of a roaring fire, comfortable on the carved settle that had been his wedding present to them.

It was cold today but there was no roaring fire and no settle. That was gone. Long since bartered for the means to keep her children fed for a few more days.

'Mistress Dickson, how are you faring?'

He strode forward, uninvited, tipping his chin and glancing sharply at the children, indicating that she should send them outside.

She gathered them closer to her, though whether for their protection or hers, she would be hard put to say.

'Moderately well, Master Carpenter thank you,' she lied.

'Aye I can see that, mistress.' His manner softened and, for a moment, he was the old Ralph, the welcome visitor. 'Then you'll not be needing this,' and from behind his back, he produced a small chicken.

She had it on the tip of her tongue to refuse but John's rake thin hands were already grasping the bird. She bent her head with a sigh, quickly stifled. For it was no gift that young John was chuckling over. The chicken would have to be paid for and it seemed that Ralph was looking for payment sooner, rather than later. His hand was hot through the threadbare material of her dress as he kneaded her shoulder, bending to whisper, 'Come. Send the children outside.'

'No Ralph I cannot. They are barely warm enough as it is. They would surely take a chill outdoors. Be patient, I pray you.' She winced as he tightened his grip.

'This once,' he breathed. 'I'll come by later,' and he stalked away without acknowledging the greetings of the children.

What a sorry state of affairs that she should be glad to see the back of Will's best friend. Wiping her hands on her apron, she called to her son, 'Come John, help me pluck this bird and get it in the pot. Mary, see if you can find some dry sticks. We'll build the fire and have chicken broth for supper.'

There had been a time when chicken broth would have met with a sniff and curled up lip but even Mary clapped her hands at the unexpected treat.

'Mother,' John blew a chicken feather off his nose, 'What's a papist brat?'

'Why, John, wherever did you hear such an expression?' Of course, she already knew the answer. What was it now, a year? Eighteen months? A long time for children to remember the old taunts but John bore new bruises every day defending something he did not understand. She struggled to find an answer, hampered by her own limited knowledge. Well a Papist is someone who supports the Pope as head of the Church.'

Puzzled, John asked, 'Do we? Did father?'

'No, not really.' Poor Will, she thought he was more in tune with the seasons than the warring Church factions.

' Then why did they hang him? And why didn't they hang Uncle Ralph and Master Farrier as well?'

'I wish I knew the answer, my son. One thing you must remember; your father was a brave and honourable man and died for doing his duty to his liege lord. He had no choice. He swore an oath of fealty to Earl Westmorland and was duty bound to answer the call to arms when it came.'

'Yes but why him? Why not the others?'

'I don't know John. I wish I did. Now, come see, you've left some feathers in near the neck. Finish plucking while I get a taper to singe the bird.'

'Mother?' John's voice was soft with sleep so she knew the question was important to him. 'Is Uncle Ralph our father, now?'

She was shocked. 'No. No. Why do you ask?'

'Well,' he was almost asleep, and probably barely aware of what he was saying. 'Well, when he comes, you and he do what you and father used to do. You know.'

Shamed and embarrassed, she sought to silence him by kissing his forehead and tucking what few covers there were more closely round him.

'Hush, child, sleep now,' and the gentle breathing told her she had succeeded.

Sitting alone by the dying fire, John's words haunted her. So the child had been awake then. It had been wrong, a sin even, but she was afraid. Afraid of being alone and friendless and Ralph had offered some comfort. For the children, there had been a rabbit here, a pigeon there, food for their stomachs. A window boarded, more warmth for their cold little bodies, but always a price to be paid and the price got steeper over the months.

As if she had summoned him with her thoughts, he stepped quietly into the glow of the fire. He didn't even speak, just grabbed her shoulders pulling her off the stool towards him.

'No Ralph,' she twisted away.

He smiled, thinking maybe she played the flirt and made to catch hold of her again.

'No. It is not right. I cannot. You must stop coming here.'

'Must I, Mistress? Then you and your whelps will surely starve.'

'That may well be so, but better that, than being held to ransom by your demands,' she hissed, then added softly, 'yet I cannot believe that you would let the children of a man you called a friend suffer because of me.'

With cold deliberation he hooked his foot under the pot and sent three day's food gushing onto the earth floor.

She flung herself forward, hoping to salvage a few dregs, but he caught her by the arm.

'I can bring another chicken tomorrow.' It was half question, half statement, and he waited, confident that she would capitulate.

She stood, head drooping for a moment, then took a step back and brought her chin up. 'No Ralph. No more. It was wrong from the start.'

'Was it, Mistress? You hardly took any persuading.'

She flushed then, in shame but also in anger. Oh, there was just enough truth in his words to hurt but he knew as well as she, it was the price he extracted to keep her children fed.

'Go back to your wife, Ralph,' she said tiredly, unwilling to continue the argument.

'Ah well, Mistress, my wife is near her time and I would not wish for my,' he paused, 'attentions,' another pause, 'to damage the bairn.'

She stiffened. 'I had not known that. You bastard!'

Surprisingly he laughed. 'You damn me, Lady? That's rare, coming from one who harboured a traitor.'

They had been speaking in whispers but their voices had risen as their words became ever more acrimonious.

'Will was no traitor, as well you know. He answered the summons of Lord Neville. You did so yourself. They could just as easily have hanged you.'

'Don't be stupid, woman. Did you never ask yourself why he was chosen?' I'll tell you why. It's because he was useless. See these hands? There's skill here. I can make things. That's why Sam Miller and Henry Farrier still live, why the village still has a baker. And why they even spared the man who butchers the kine.'

'No!' The reedy screech startled them both. John must have heard Ralph's bitter tirade because he launched himself, fists flailing, at Ralph's legs. He wore a thin nightshift and looked light as a moth in the dying glow of the fire. Ralph had the grace to look embarrassed, side-stepping to avoid the rush of the enraged child.

As he did so his foot caught in the handle of the upturned broth pot and he fell heavily, his head cracking against the hearth-stone.

She clasped John tight. They clung together, expecting Ralph to get up. John was shivering and so was she. They waited but he did not stir. They waited longer and still he did not move.

Putting the child from her, she knelt by Ralph's side. In the final, flickering embers she could see a dark pool under Ralph's head. She touched it lightly and licked at her finger, tasting the salty, metallic flavour of blood. She bent closer, listening for the sound of the heartbeat or the whisper of a breath but there was none.

'John,' she said keeping her voice calm and authoritative, 'Go wake Mary. Get dressed, both of you; your warmest clothes, and hurry.'

Draping her one and only shawl around her shoulders she went and stood in the doorway.

Dawn was a pale sliver of salvation in the East. The stars were fading and would soon be gone.

By the time the last one had blinked out, she hoped that she, and her children would be well on the way to sanctuary at Durham Cathedral.

THOU SHALT WANT ERE I WANT,' the motto of the Cranstouns, could well have been the motto of any of the families of reivers on either side of the border between England and Scotland. Theirs was a situation initially brought about by the politics of the 1500s which set family against family. It became a mode of life to war against one another for supplies of food often in the form of livestock. It was customary for them to sing ballads about their heroes. The characters in this story are fictitious.

'THOU SHALT WANT ERE I WANT'
Betty Bone

A hundred men are assembled
By the Lang, Jagged Stane o' the moor
A hundred swells to three hundred or more.
A body of horsemen outside the law.
But nae sign o' Robbie the Red.

Satisfied that the horse beneath him had responded well to his guidance over the moor, Robbie felt encouraged about the next part of the journey. Since he had acquired the horse on a previous raid, they had built up a rapport and now he and Cutlass moved as one. A stench particular to evening time rose as they neared the boggy land. Cutlass picked her way across the squelching sleck without faltering. Robbie patted her approvingly and Cutlass gave an answering snort, Robbie was assured that all would be well. For a reiver on his way to a raid, it was essential to have confidence in his mount. This would be doubly so on the return journey. Escape from pursuers depended on a good horse. Robbie hoped they wouldn't turn out the hounds. Although he would never admit to it, the sound of those baying animals made his blood curdle.

It was not yet dark but Mary had already lit the candles and set one in Donald's room. She could hardly believe he was already seven years old. Had her husband, Fergus, been at home he would have insisted that Donald went to bed without a light.

'Mak' a man o' him,' Fergus would have said. 'Times're hard. Nae room for weaklings in this world.'

Times were hard but Donald was still a small child.

'Time enough, before manhood.'

She placed all but one of the remaining candles on the long, heavy table which ran down the centre of the sparsely furnished room. Walking to the window that was barely more than a niche, she set down the last candle. She fingered her beads. It might have been a prayer to atone for a sin not yet committed as well as for those of the past. Out on the moor, Robbie viewed the candle with pleasure and urged Cutlass to quicken her stride.

At their meeting place, the Lang Jagged Stone, the reivers were eating. Soon they would be settling down for some rest before moving on. At intervals, the buzz of talk was broken by raucous laughter as bawdy jokes were passed among the men. But for one of their number, it was no time for joking.

'Ha' ye seen Robbie?' Jamie almost certain of the reply, glowered as he spoke. He was already selecting those men he was to use as an advanced corps.

'No, and we're no likely to see him yet a while. I spied a light in Mary's window as we passed. Fergus must be on his travels,' one of the men offered.

The implication was not lost on Jamie. He could have thought of better nights for Mary to take Robbie to her bed and his annoyance was coloured by frustration — not merely because Robbie was delayed.

Jamie didn't hear the remark which followed from within the group as he concentrated on his recruitment. There was little doubt that it centred on Mary and Robbie. Whatever it was, it brought more loud, coarse laughter which Jamie heard with pain. Soon it would be time to take a little rest.

Mary waited until Robbie had dismounted in the yard, before going again to Donald's room to check that he was sleeping.

'Will ye come now?'

She was smiling as she fetched Robbie in and they stood for a while watching their sleeping child. The lingering with Mary took rather longer than Robbie had intended and by the time he reached the meeting place, only scant evidence that the reivers had been there, remained. Robbie looked for the name scooped in the soil, at the foot of the stone, for the customary guide for late comers. It was there, the tail of the last letter curving in the direction he was to take.

'Howay noo, Cutlass, see what ye can do!' They set off at lightning speed, horse and rider in unison, each conveying to the other the enjoyment of the ride, Robbie alight by the thoughts of what lay ahead. Long before the assembled horsemen reached the spot from which they would make their final thrust, Robbie had joined Jamie at the head of one of the columns of men.

'Ye took yer time.' Jamie's bad mood was still on him.

'Could nae be helped. I'm here the noo.'

'If Fergus ever catches ye, ye'll be in fearsome trouble.'

'An de ye ken its no yer business. Who cares aboot Fergus anyway?' Jamie had to admit that not many people did, but he was in no mood to agree with his friend.

'And what about her. Ha' ye thought aboot that? The other women here aboots could drum her awa' frae home if they felt so inclined. Then what?' Deliberately he did not mention Mary by name. 'Besides,' he went on, 'ye should ha' had the raid in mind. I would'na be takin' such risks.'

This wasn't quite true for Jamie would have given a great deal for the favours of Mary. He had known her as a child. He had admired her as a blossoming young woman. Jamie had been deeply angered that Mary had been forced into a marriage to relieve her father Harold of his gambling debts. Ten years before, Fergus, a man of almost Harold's own age, had defeated him in an extended game of cards. The young Mary had been used as a pledge in that last terrible session between them. Mary had never shown more than friendship towards Jamie. Nor had he ever found in himself the courage to offer her more. His courage and leadership was limited to what he knew best, raiding for food and supplies. In truth Jamie envied Robbie. He was a fine looking man who got the name of Robbie the Red because of the neat, auburn beard he sported. Self assured, he could laugh in the face of danger, meet that danger on his own terms and come away victorious. Above that, he had the energy and courage of two men. This presence earned him the admiration of many. Yet because of this very popularity, Jamie was certain that Robbie must have created jealous enemies.

So the two men rode on in silence. When at last Jamie's mood softened, he began to discuss the conduct and strategy of the raid. Robbie listened respectfully, only occasionally interrupting to verify a particular point. The plan was to take as many sheep as they could drive away. Kine were as important. Food was running so low and where there were forests, the autumn leaves were already lying thick and sodden under the trees.

'We'll need good stocks te tide us ower the winter. The horses A'll leave wi' yea.' They needed to be selective so far as horses were concerned. That was Robbie's particular domain. 'A've allocated a hundred men for ye.'

Soon they would reach the point whence the raid would take place. Two more miles and they spread out to begin their tasks.

There was a protest from the animals as they were disturbed, as well as the shouts of the reivers themselves, as they charged about to get the work done. As was inevitable, there were casualties and some men were captured. When Robbie was satisfied, he was on his way with his own company of men driving on the horses. They made a good distance and he was fairly certain that there were no hostile pursuers. It had been a good night's work but just as he was beginning to feel more relaxed. Robbie realised that Cutlass was slowing down and he needed to dismount. Her leg was gammy, and with the bond between man and horse, on no account would he continue riding. He knew of a cave half a mile to the west. He could hide out there, where he could see to her and carry on when he could. Detailing his best man to take command, Robbie put his plan into operation. Just inside the entrance to the cave, he comforted Cutlass and with dawn breaking, inspected the ailing fetlock. Thankful that it was nothing more than a stone that was grieving the animal, he saw to it and took her deeper into the cave to recover before completing the journey.

Several hours later the two set off for home, both walking at a steady pace. Robbie wanted to be sure that Cutlass was ready to take his weight. A scuffle in the green bents and the cry of disturbed curlews momentarily startled Cutlass. Robbie patted her and spoke soothingly to her, but not for long. From a hiding place they must have occupied for hours, a group of men sprang out. The horse reared, caught one of them with her hoof and the man went down. Another raised a weapon and was about to strike Cutlass. Pinned down, Robbie called out. 'Away wi ye, Cutlass, away.' Eyes blazing, the frightened animal obeyed.

Robbie's courage did not desert him. He fought a brave fight but even he was no match for the remaining five men from the ambush.

* * *

'A stray? A stray, ye say?' Fergus, returning from his days in Alnwick, was talking to his stable boy.

'Aye, Maister. A've given him hay and water.'

'Whisht a'll talk te ye tomorrow. A'll away te ma bed. It's been a long road.'

Willie the stable boy was surprised but thankful that Fergus had taken so little interest in the horse, which he had found wandering in the yard, earlier that day. Willie recognised the horse from Robbie's visits. Forming the obvious conclusion that some misfortune had sent it back alone, he had alerted Mary. Since then she had paced the room for hours, frequently looking through the window. At intervals, she ran her beads through her fingers, murmuring as she did so. She was nursing a forlorn hope. Robbie did not return that day or ever.

The day after Fergus returned, he had stayed in bed. At one point he had called out and asked for Donald to be taken to him. Despite his apparent harshness, Fergus was fond of Donald, unaware that the child was not his. What he owned would one day belong to Donald. Mary would never reveal the truth. If she had made sacrifices, at least her son could reap any benefit, by allowing the situation to remain as it was. But even that satisfaction was denied her.

Whatever disease Fergus had carried home was swift to kill and Donald as well as Fergus were dead within days.

In the weeks that followed, Jamie did his best to comfort Mary whilst he, too, mourned the loss of his friend. Often he would call to find her staring from the window. She became a tragic figure in a very short time. Jamie wondered how long she would survive.

'Not long,' he thought and his fears were quickly realised. Soon he was mourning the loss of Mary, too.

* * *

Stories such as this hold a fascination for local inhabitants and visitors alike but it seemed to me, that since they happened so long ago they were embellished legends, rather than pure fact. Even so, they added that certain magic to an area, which already held a great attraction for me.

Back in the 1970s we liked to hitch a caravan onto the car and were then free to go as we pleased. Often we travelled up the

West Coast of Scotland and sometimes out to the islands. In those days there wasn't the same necessity to find a caravan site as there is now. As we lived in Durham, the border country made a perfect stopping place for the night, especially if we hadn't set off until after the day's work. It was not yet dark when we parked the caravan. Although quite late and with the moon rising, we could still see daylight in the sky ahead.

I had a restless nature and on the first night of a holiday, always found it difficult to wind down from the preparation I had made before. We decided to take a short walk. When we returned to the caravan, I almost stumbled over a pile of stones. No harm done, the incident was forgotten almost as soon as it had happened. Even after going to bed, sleep still seemed as far away as ever. It would have been unfair to Simon to continue reading, so I put out the light and lay watching the moon through a small gap in the curtains.

'What's that noise?' Quickly I sat up, pulling my curtain aside. 'There's something stirring out there, Simon.' I said into the now moonlit space.

'There's something stirring in here!' he said. 'It feels like being in a boat. Do go to sleep! We've a long drive tomorrow.'

There was no reply to anything else I said and I assumed that Simon was asleep. It wasn't long before snoring confirmed it. I continued to look out onto the moonlit moor. At one stage I gently opened the window, expecting the air to be fresh and clear but it smelt unbelievably damp and musty, so that I moved to slide the window shut.

How hadn't I seen her before? A slight figure. Her hair fell about her shoulders. A momentary gust of wind showed that it hung almost to her waist. For a while she stood totally still. Her arm was raised, bent at the elbow, so that her hand must have been at eye level. That attitude suggested that she was looking for someone. Another gust of wind bore on it a faint sob and then another. When at last I saw her move she seemed to float across my vision. I was quite transfixed. She reached the cairn, picked up a stone and placed it on the others. I heard it slide before it found a resting place. It was a situation so real, yet so unreal. For a fleeting moment, I thought of waking Simon to prove what I was witnessing. Then I knew I shouldn't. I must not!

She stood again, so still, except for the movement of her hands.

They were now together, but not clasped, just above her waist, moving gently.

Then we heard it! Both she and I. I saw her head move so that her chin jerked upwards as mine did and instinctively I knew, that this sound in the night, would bring us both pleasure. Faintly at first and then more clearly, the pad of hooves, picking their way across the soft ground. Then onto firmer ground and soon horse and rider were within our sight. When he jumped from his mount I shared as I was meant to share, moments of sheer delight. Moments which it had taken centuries to reach. He lifted her onto the horse and they moved towards the cairn. A small boy was lifted onto the horse's back beside her. Knowing well by now that I was not an intruder, I continued to watch, as the three went off into the night. They reached the higher ground. As they moved out of sight, I heard the wind rustling through the grasses. It seemed to raise its pitch, but it was not a sad, cold wind I heard. Listening to its remarkable soothing, I experienced an inward peace, which, until then I had never known.

In 1594 John, the 7th Lord Lumley, keen to demonstrate his noble lineage decided to assemble memorials to his ancestors. He began by pilfering two from Durham Cathedral, stating that they were 14th Century predecessors, though their armour dates from much earlier. He collected fourteen, some contemporary that were mutilated to give the appearance of age and to enable them to fit in available space. Carved in Frosterly marble, they can be seen along the wall of the North aisle in the Parish Church of St. Mary and St. Cuthbert, Chester-le-Street.
But what did the family think of the idea...?

PURLOINED PROGENITORS
Sandra Salmon

'I agree husband mine, that a man needs a hobby but what are they?

Yes I can see that, thank you but what are they for? The hall? Garden ornaments?

You're going to put them where?

Have you completely lost your mind? They're nothing to do with us. Who's going to believe that they're your ancestors?

They don't even look like you. This one's quite handsome.

Where does he come from?

Durham Cathedral!

Now I know you've gone quite mad. Do you think nobody will recognise it? Take it back.

Look, John. I don't want to spend any more time running this place alone while you fester in some prison or other. Remember that narrow escape over trying to marry Norfolk off to Mary of Scotland, poor dear child? Did it teach you nothing? I know it was twenty years ago but if you think I've got a long memory, you'll find Church and State have even longer ones and purloining artefacts from one of their centres of religion is probably punishable by execution.

Anyway you'll need more than those two, if you intend to fill the North aisle.

Oh, you've thought of that, have you? Dare I ask what your solution is? Suicide?

You're having some made locally.

Well don't stint yourself.
I'm sure they come cheaper by the dozen.'

17th Century

In 1667 a duty was imposed on every chaldron (a measurement equalling approximately 23 hundredweight) of coal, shipped from Newcastle, for the purpose of restoring Parish churches destroyed by the Great Fire of London in 1666.

THE MORE THINGS CHANGE THE MORE THEY STAY THE SAME
(Alphonse Karr; 1808 - 1890)
John Gamblin

The Arctic honed blade of the east wind instantly beheaded its own white horses scurrying across the tiny harbour on the edge of the Tyne estuary. Andrew Brevert, mariner turned ship-owner, shrugged the collar of his woollen overcoat tighter around raw ears, as he steered a narrow course along the unfenced quayside. He turned a corner, grateful for the protection of the neglected timber-framed houses, but impatient with the pale moonlight weakly illuminating fading numbers, painted on rough hewn doors. He finally found his destination and, irritably, gave the door a resounding blow with the heavy handle of his stout hazel stick. It was opened immediately and the odour of perspiring bodies spilled into the night.

Doorway formalities completed, Andrew joined the meeting. The low room concentrated the acrid tobacco haze into a throat-searing mixture. He nodded greetings to those with whom he was acquainted and cast curious glances at those few with whom he was not. The heat of humanity encased him, in stifling contrast to the outdoor chill he had just left and he struggled for enough space to remove his heavy coat.

The drumming of an ale jug on a bare oak table halted the hubbub. Andrew recognised the Chairman as a coal owner named Wilkinson.

'Gentlemen! We are here because we all recognise that this new duty on coal will affect each one of us to some extent.' Agreement rippled over the assembly.

'Not Parliament I'd say, but the Cabal,' a voice shouted.

'Aye, but the Cabal does nothing without a nod from the King,' argued another.

'The King would not impose a duty on Newcastle only', interrupted a third, 'we're Royalist. Always have been.'

'Aye', yet another voice agreed, 'the King would put his duty on the bloody Parliamentarians and they're in Sunderland.'

'Would anyone do that and raise less than a quarter of what he'll get off the Tyne?' asked Andrew mockingly. 'Listen! Kings are just ordinary people who happen to have a crown and ordinary people get what they can where they can.' His words covered the buzz of conversation with a deadening blanket.

'I think we should have no more talk in that vein, Mr. Brevert.' the Chairman said, trying to regain control.

'I agree, Sir. What we should be talking of, is the purpose for which this duty is to be used.'

'The people of London are in great need after their disastrous fire, Sir. Of that we are all aware', said Wilkinson, coldly.

'Indeed we are. But, are we aware that the people who produce this coal are in great need also?' A dozen people to a room is common in our mining villages. Can London be any worse than that?'

'You object to helping London, Mr. Brevert? Is that your protest?'

'Exactly, but not only my protest. You all protest and do nothing. I don't want to pay this duty any more than you, but I think, if we have to pay it in the North, let it be spent in the North and tax Londoners to rebuild London.'

Murmurings of hesitant approval were stifled by a man standing at the rear of the room. He was dressed expensively and with a stronger sense of fashion than was normally found in North East England. His round face had a homely look, totally at odds with the razor edge to his voice.

'Take care, Sir, that your thoughts do not lead you into irresponsible action. You may very well find that the authority which makes the law, has enough force to impose it.'

'Perhaps so', retorted Andrew, 'and who, might I enquire, gives me the benefit of such invaluable information?'

'One you should listen to', replied the stranger, 'since it is his report which will be read in London,' and, looking neither right nor left, he departed.

The nervous silence disintegrated into sixty voices speaking simultaneously. Andrew, recognising that the meeting had been expertly demolished, gathered his coat and cane and left.

Grateful for the smell of the open sea after the steaming meeting room, Andrew turned briskly onto the quayside into a scramble of bodies. The quarter moon dimly lit a man with his back against the wall, defending himself with foot and fist against two others attempting to bring him down. As Andrew took in the scene, one of the attackers obtained a grip on a flailing leg and jerked his victim to the ground. Giving neither thought nor hesitation Andrew swung his stick, delivering a blow squarely on the temple of the nearer of the two who was unconscious before touching the ground. Surprised, the second assailant reacted slowly before turning to run from this new threat. Andrew swung at the running legs. In missing, his cane passed between the fleeing knees, tripping the would be escapee who disappeared head first over the edge of the quay to the sound of a splash.

'I am most grateful to you, Sir. Without your intervention I was finished.'

Andrew recognised the incisive tones of the stranger at the meeting. 'I would do no less for anyone in such a predicament.'

'Ah! I hear Mr. Brevert's voice if I'm not mistaken. Allow me to introduce myself, Sir. My name is Lauderdale.' The two shook hands and Lauderdale continued, 'Would you dine with me, Mr. Brevert, so that I may properly show my gratitude?'

'I fancy that would be an interesting meal indeed, Mr. Lauderdale, but, with regret, I must decline. There is a prior engagement.'

'Pity, the next time we meet, perhaps.'

'Yes, perhaps.'

'Before you go, Mr. Brevert! Please don't do anything rash. I do know that the duty on sea coal has the highest authority and it will be levied. Any resistance, from whatever quarter, will be removed by whatever means are necessary.'

'Why coal, Mr. Lauderdale?'

'Because the profit is big enough to stand it. Anyway, those who profit will only pass on the cost. In the end it is the people who will pay.'

'I understand your meaning but dislike your code, Mr. Lauderdale'

'Don't become caught in the middle, my friend. I would be powerless to help you', and, for the second time that night, Lauderdale turned and walked away.

Immersed in his thoughts Andrew walked to the house he had visited since his teenage years and could have found blindfold. William Hubble, former First Mate to Andrew's father, grinned at his visitor. The ice blue eyes set in a weather grizzled face were full of lively curiosity. His body, despite its sixty something years was still lean and hard.

'A hot grog is what you need, Andy my lad.'

'When did you not have the right answer, William?' Andrew laughed.

The pair occupied high backed chairs, placed to enjoy the glowing fire. The room contained no furniture that was not essential for the needs of a single man. What there was, however, reflected the character of the man in every polished surface. William broke the comfortable silence which accompanied their rum.

'Now then, tell me what your problem is.'

'You're sure I have one?' said his visitor with a smile.

'I know you as well as I knew your father. Shall I give you a start? What would you reply to a question about tax on sea coal?'

'You're right, you old fox! William, I see no reason why the North should be punished because London had a fire.'

'They reckon 13,000 houses got destroyed. That's a lot of homeless people, Andy.'

'This tax is not about houses. I could stomach it, if it was. No, this is about replacing parish churches.'

'Aye, there was a lot of them went up as well.'

'And we're expected to pay for fifty of them. Aye and St. Paul's as well', said the younger man angrily.

William shook his head, 'I think you're going to have to make the best of it, young fella. Laws are made to suit those who make them and our laws are made in London.'

'Laws are made to be got around.'

'That's trouble talk, Andrew.'

I've been told that already tonight. Listen William, the Dutch war is over and the North Sea is safe. This is no time for sitting back and watching profit drain away.'

'You've got something stuck in your throat. Spit it out and let's have a look.'

'The law says: Duty on sea coal coming out of the Port of Newcastle.'

'Aye, Lad. I know.'

'Right! I'm taking my coal out of Sunderland.'

William said anxiously, 'The plague's in Sunderland.'

'There hasn't been a case for six weeks but that's why there are berths for the asking. I bought two yesterday.'

'And you call me an old fox. It might work.'

'It will work, believe me. I will sell my coal cheaper than the Tyne, because it's only a matter of time before they have to raise their price to cover the duty. I've seen plans for a wagonway the length of the Wear and a chaldron on wheels that can drop two and a half tons of coal straight into the hold. We will load a ship in less than a day without having to pay a single keel boat.'

'What do you want me for then, Andy? You seem to have all the ends tied together.'

'Find me two more vessels, old man. With six ships we can have one loading and one unloading every day of the week.'

* * *

Four years later early spring sunshine was swelling bright new buds on the trees in Windsor Great Park, while thrushes and finches chirruped courtship from the treetops. This sense of pastoral bliss enveloped the King, strolling with three members of, what had become known as, his Cabal. This unofficial government preferred to have their discussions away from prying Parliamentary ears. The King's spaniels frolicking around their strolling feet would give ample warning of any unwelcome presence. Lord Clifford, watching carefully, saw that his Sovereign's features were relaxed, despite the heat in the conversation.

'We have had enough talk of divorce, Clifford. It is quite out of the question.'

'Sire!' interposed the Duke of Buckingham 'Do you not see that if you die without issue your brother could cause another civil war - Protestant fighting Catholic?'

'I am not convinced of that. However, on the subject of issue, what if Mistress Gwynne should give me a son?'

'You would not marry Mistress Gwynne, Sire?' queried Lords Ashley and Clifford, anxiety apparent in both voices.

The King roared with laughter, 'Marry Nell? Not in a thousand years. She is a comfortable bed partner, it's sure but then, so are many others.'

His companions smiled understandingly. The King turned his gaze in the direction of the Castle.

'Here comes Lauderdale. He disapproves of Nell, so let us finish this conversation quickly. The point is that she carries my child, the others do not. Now, if she gives me a son, where would he stand in succession?'

'Nowhere, Sire, with respect.' Clifford replied firmly.

'As I thought. Then I must give his future some consideration. Ah! Lord Lauderdale, welcome.'

The newcomer bowed.

'Tell us, Lauderdale, have you found the source of this cheap product flooding our coal market?'

'I have, Sire.'

'Good. I placed my trust wisely.'

Lauderdale nodded, 'It is supplied by a ship-owner named Brevert, your Majesty.'

'Brevert? Never heard of him.'

'No, Sire. I can understand that.'

'How does he sell it so cheaply?'

'He loads and sails from a duty free port, Sire.'

'Then we must close that loophole.'

'That is one way, Sire. Alternatively one could impose an unloading tax.'

'Very clever, Lauderdale. See to it.'

'However, Sire, we should also take into consideration that an unloading tax would be expensive to collect, and the blame for higher coal prices could then fall on your Majesty's shoulders.'

'Oh! Get on with it, Lauderdale. I know you. You have something up your sleeve.'

'There is the third way, Sire.'

'Ah! The third way? Explain that, Sir.'

'Brevert, Sire, has only eight vessels plying out of Sunderland and they carry the largest part of the sea coal coming out of that port. Newcastle, on the other hand, has over a hundred ships in the trade.'

'Well?'

'Imposing a duty on the Port of Sunderland would not greatly increase Revenue and, taking away from the poor a source of cheaper coal, could result in a loss of your Majesty's popularity.'

'The poor? What can the poor do about it?'

'At risk of your displeasure, Sire, there is a swell of opinion against your Majesty's association with Mistress Gwynne, to which it would be unwise to add.'

'And your advice is, Lord Lauderdale?' said the King icily.

'Do not impose more sea coal duty, Sire. Very soon London will have no further need of this money. The Newcastle Burghers will be expecting the tax to be revoked but it may be that your Majesty will have other commitments. Newcastle is, after all, now used to paying the levy.'

'Quite so. Other commitments, eh? That is very likely', said the King, thoughtfully, 'you may have a good point there Lauderdale but what should we do with this scoundrel Brevert, eh?'

'Award him a knighthood, Sire, for services to the poor. That way the poor will see that you truly care for their well being.'

In 1999, worried about the effect on inflation of rapidly increasing property prices in London, the authorities began a programme of Interest Rate rises, disregarding the adverse effect of these on the remainder of the Country.

Andrew Mills, a simpleton, was found guilty of murdering three children. Buried in Kirk Merrington, the inscription on their tomb read: 'Here lie the bodies of John, Jane and Elizabeth, children of Louis and Margaret Brass, murdered on 25th January 1683, by Andrew Mills their father's servant of which he was found guilty.' Andrew's father disagreed with the verdict and spent the next twenty years removing the word 'guilty' with the tip of his walking stick. The tomb was restored in 1757 and the epitaph changed but the groove is still visible.

SCRATCHING
Sandra Salmon

Father, go home.
Day after day, scratching.
Don't you hear? Can't you see?
Day after day, scratching.

Your faith binds me here.
Day after day scratching.
Let them rest. Set me free.
Day after day, scratching.

It is only a word.
Day after day scratching.
Give them peace. Let me be.
Day after day, scratching.

Tiny bodies, grave cold.
Day after day, scratching.
Did I kill? Was it me?
Father, go home.

≈ 18TH CENTURY ≈

In 1755 Jedediah Buxton was at Newcastle. He could neither read nor write but performed the most difficult arithmetical calculations. Presumably, the 'Newcastle Journal', founded fourteen years earlier, sent someone to report on this event.

THE HUMAN CALCULATOR
Eve Stockmann

'Can I see you for a minute, Mr. Curtis?' The young man had worked for Isaac Thompson almost since he first published the *Newcastle Journal*, long enough to be able to tell shades of mood even from a short request. Whatever his editor had in store for him today, it promised to be exciting.

'Bring any work you've done on Jedediah Buxton.'

Wrong. Jedediah Buxton was not exciting. Richard Curtis had had several attempts this morning at writing an article about him. He never got any further than: 'Jedediah Buxton's performances in arithmetical calculation have been looked upon by the Royal Society and several persons of distinction. They declared them to be the most surprising, as well as the most curious ever to be performed in England.' He had no trouble going on in the same vein, but who wanted to read it? He needed a different angle.

Isaac barely left Richard enough time to enter the room.

'Do you know whom I met last night at the King's Head?' He didn't pause long enough for an answer. 'Jedediah Buxton's father. What a pompous little man! He claims the credit for having developed his son's talents and is very keen to benefit from them. Anyway, the Buxtons are staying in the King's Head.'

'Which, of course, you knew, Sir.'

'Somebody brought it to my attention.' A wry smile went over Isaac's face. 'Mr. Buxton had been told that I was there. So, of course, he sought me out. He probably never misses an opportunity to have the unique talents of his son brought to the attention of a wider audience. But, listen to this: as the night progressed, Mr. Buxton had a little too much to drink, and then blurted out what he really thinks of his son.'

Richard expected some saucy tale. Giving free rein to his imagination, he conjured up the picture of a fat little man with a purple nose - Mr. Buxton - who had found his son in bed with one of the servant girls at the King's Head.

'Do you know anything about Mr. Buxton, senior?' Isaac's question brought Richard's thoughts back to the office.

'Only what you know already.'

'All this about having taught his son? Believe me, he never taught his son anything. Jedediah can neither read nor write!'

'But his arithmetic ... ? Surely, Mr. Buxton ...'

'William Buxton only thinks of himself.' Isaac Thompson's voice sizzled with indignation. 'I do believe he never even liked his son - it's the way he speaks about him. Seems that he lost any inclination to teach him, when it turned out that Jedediah was different to other children. Calls him a half-wit and ridicules him for lacking a proper profession.'

'But that hardly appears to be Jedediah's fault,' Richard dared to interrupt.

'Exactly,' Isaac agreed passionately. 'I think we have to cut Mr. William Buxton down to size.' He paused to look at Richard and was satisfied when he read approval in his face. 'Just imagine people's reaction when they learn that Jedediah is self-taught,' he chuckled. 'Go and talk to him this morning, while his father is still incapacitated. See what you make of him.'

Jedediah greeted Richard with a nervous smile. 'I am sorry, my father is not very well. He usually deals with this sort of thing. I am not very good at it.'

Richard took an immediate liking to the shy little man, whose weather beaten face and rough hands were testimony of his work as a farm labourer.

'But you are better at numbers than anyone else!'

His face lit up. 'Oh, numbers, they're all right. Do you want to ask me questions in arithmetic?'

The change in Jedediah's demeanor, as he solved one mathematical problem after another, was startling. His eyes which, before, had shifted aimlessly from one object to another, were now firmly fixed ahead; indecisiveness gave way to assertiveness, nervousness to self-confidence. He worked out the square root of 56,295,009 before Richard had time to repeat the number, and did not take much longer to calculate the product of 56,974 multiplied by 4,397. So it went on. It occurred to Richard that Jedediah could easily make up answers, if there was nobody to check their correctness, but he scolded himself almost immediately for doubting him.

'How do you do this, Jedediah? Is there a trick?'

'No, no trick. Numbers fascinate me - size, length, anything like that.'

'Your father must be very proud of you.'

Jedediah turned his head as if to make sure that his father was out of earshot. 'I don't really think so. I make him very angry - always have done.'

'Why do you think that?'

'He thinks that I don't listen to him, and that's something he cannot abide. But you know, the more people talk, the more I count their words and then I don't hear what they say.'

'Ah, I see. The angrier your father gets ... '

'... the more he says ...'

'... and the more you count, without taking a word in. - I bet, he doesn't like that.'

Jedediah hesitantly joined in Richard's giggle. He had not known many people in his life who had treated him as an equal, and definitely not many people whom he trusted the way he did his new-found friend.

Back at the office, Richard assured Mr. Thompson that he shared his opinion about Mr. Buxton. 'I have not even set eyes on the man yet, but I get the impression that Jedediah needs a more sympathetic champion of his cause.'

The hall was crowded when Jedediah started his public performance under the auspices of the great mathematician, Mr. Robert Harrison. The audience could hardly believe the speed and ease with which Jedediah multiplied and divided numbers, which they could not even pronounce. After a while Mr. Harrison asked more unusual questions.

'How many hair's breadths, at 48 to an inch, would reach from Newcastle to London?'

The people gasped. How could anyone answer that? Jedediah had told Richard that he could stride over a field and measure its size exactly, with no other means whatsoever. But to give such an enormous distance in hair's breadths? And to calculate it all in his head? Surely that was impossible! Richard looked across to Jedediah's father, whom he had met earlier. William Buxton sat, fully confident that his son could give the correct reply, but he was waiting to claim the praise.

The answer came in less than three minutes, '833,310,720.'

Everyone was cheering and clapping their hands with delight, expressions of astonishment were interspersed with shouts for more.

'All right, one more. Are you ready, Mr. Buxton?'

Jedediah nodded. Richard had studied his friend's expression closely and recognised the same sense of direction and purpose as the day before, and he also knew that Jedediah had banished all but figures from his mind.

'Please tell me how many guineas, placed edgeways, would pave a turnpike road, nine yards wide, from Newcastle to London. Assume that each piece is an inch broad and 1/15 of an inch thick.'

A hush fell over the hall. Nobody dared move for fear of breaking Jedediah's concentration, only William Buxton started to prepare his smile. Again it took Jedediah no longer than three minutes to calculate the solution.

'84,372,710,400.'

All eyes now rested on Mr. Harrison, who looked at the calculation which he had previously done in writing. Eventually he gave an approving nod and the hall exploded with shouts of 'brilliant', 'fantastic', 'incredible'. Richard looked at Jedediah, whose mind still seemed to be with his figures and who appeared completely unaffected by what was going on around him, and then at his father who was bowing to the crowd, wearing a well rehearsed, oily smile.

'Excuse me, Jedediah. One more question!'

Jedediah nodded.

'How often has your father called you a half-wit?'

'12,937 times,' the answer came immediately.

'And when was the last time?'

'Yesterday.'

The oily smile had dried up on Mr. Buxton's face as he hurriedly left the hall, followed by a roar of laughter.

Keelboats were a familiar sight on the rivers Tyne and Wear from the early Sixteenth Century to the middle of the Nineteenth Century. They were a link between the coal and the large ships, which were unable to sail to the point of supply upstream from the Tyne Bridge. Oval in shape and with a blunt nose, they were propelled down river from spouts or collection points to the mouth by means of oars and a square sail. The huddock or small cabin was the only refuge where the Captain or one of his crew of two could shelter from poor weather. Very much ahead of their time, the keelmen had built and supported a hospital. After the coming of steam transport and the installation of staithes, the keelmen and their craft were no longer part of the river scene.

DRESS OPTIONAL
Betty Bone

As I came thro' Sandgate,
Thro' Sandgate thro' Sandgate.
As I came thro' Sangate,
I heard a lassie sing.

Chorus

Oh weel may the keel row,
The keel row,
The keel row.
Oh weel may the keel row
That my laddie's in.

He wears a blue bonnet,
Blue bonnet, blue bonnet.
He wears a blue bonnet.
A dimple in his chin.

It was early when Johnnie arrived at his keel. There was nothing odd about that. Johnnie always arrived early. Very early.

He was about to set down his basket. In it were a loaf of bread, a joint of fatty meat and the inevitable bottle of beer, his food for the next twelve to fifteen hours. He paused. Someone had arrived ahead of him. In fact some two would be more correct. They sat huddled together in the huddock of his keel. Johnnie, albeit oversized and bullnecked, found it difficult enough to squeeze in there alone to shelter from the bad weather. For two people to find enough room was unbelievable. Johnnie refrained from asking what they were doing. That was self-evident.

'Who are you?' was much more appropriate. In this Johnnie had stepped outside his normal mode of speech, as he occasionally did with strangers.

'Me - a - Umberto.   He - a - Sam.'

'Why noo, meaumberto an' heasama', ah think yud berrer stop tryin' ter mak' a fool o' me. Howay oot o' there.' If the intruders didn't understand his dialect, his gestures were unmistakable.

It proved to be quite difficult for the strangers to do as he asked, wedged as they were. It seemed to Johnnie that they took several minutes before they could extricate themselves from what had apparently been a cosy position. He suspected that it wasn't just the slight movement of the boat, as the water lapped against the quayside, which made him wince.

Seeing that Johnnie had noticed Umberto's discomfort, Sam spoke revealing his rich, Northumbrian burr.

'Umberto's hurt his foot'. We were just having a rest. Sorry. We'll go now.'

Despite his burly appearance, Johnnie had the soft heart that is quite often a characteristic of oversized men. His initial irritation quickly disappeared.

'Ya'd berrer si'doon agyen,' he said to Umberto. Sam translated.

Johnnie continued, 'Why noo Aa might just be able ter 'elp yer there but er...'

Johnnie was looking at their clothes. They were very peculiar. Little did he know, but the other two men were having the same thoughts about his. They were an oddly assorted trio. A flannel suit, fastened at the knee and blue knee-length stockings was the mode of dress of the keelmen and Johnnie was no exception. Sam wore a garment that appeared to made of hessian, and Umberto, a Roman soldier's uniform, minus the helmet.

It was while Johnnie was formulating a plan to help, that the peedee, a twelve year old, who worked on the keel, arrived.

Johnnie greeted him with, 'By, yer mother's getten yer oot soon this mornun,' Tommy.'

'Er... Er... aye.' Tommy's reply was faltering because he couldn't quite believe what he saw. Discretion not being one of Tommy's characteristics, he asked, in an overloud voice.

'Who are they then? Warra funny luk'n crew.'

Umberto, unable to understand a word, was conscious of being viewed with curiosity. He pointed in Sam's direction.

'He - a - Sam.' Then spreading out his fingers and turning both hands inwards towards his own chest, he patted out the rhythm as he said, 'Me - a - Umberto.' He nodded vigorously and smiled, concluding with the air of someone who had just performed a great aria, awaiting applause.

Tommy looked thoughtful for a few seconds. He was even more confused. 'We've nivva' had a umberto woork'n on the keel afore.'

Then thinking politeness was called for. 'Pleased ter meet yer, like.' Turning his attention to Johnnie, 'what are they ganna do?'

During this time Johnnie was thinking, so the question remained unanswered. By then Tommy's curiosity was aroused even further. This time Tommy spoke more slowly. Even he had recognised that there was a communication difficulty.

'Where - de - you,' he pointed at the men, 'live?'

'We live in lotsa place and in lotsa times.' Umberto looked pleased with himself, that he had understood the question.

Johnnie wasn't really listening to the conversation at that point. Even so, he was aware of Umberto's florid mode of expression.

Sam came to the rescue and offered, 'Once we lived at Vindolanda, then at Corbridge. Since then we move about.' Again the lovely Northumbrian burr was in evidence.

Tommy tried to look as though he had understood but he hadn't heard of Vindolanda. 'Corbridge?' No, it wasn't a bridge he'd heard of. The only bridges he knew of were those that crossed the Tyne. And the Tyne to him, was that stretch of water which was relative to Newcastle and the immediate area. The Tyne might well have had its source at Dunston spouts. Like Johnnie, his geographical knowledge extended little further than Sandgate.

Johnnie was ready to put his plan into operation and he was in luck. Foggy Brown was just passing along the quayside with his hand-cart.

'Foggy ha' yer finished wi' yer cart fer a bit?'

Foggy didn't take too long to agree to loan the handcart. Then Johnnie spoke to Tommy. 'Ha ya, got some spare troosers handy at home an' mebbee some socks.' Tommy lived very close to where the keels were moored.

'Aye, wha' for?'

'Gan an' fetch them. A'm ganna run up ter the hospital wi' Bert here,' said Johnnie, cutting Umberto's name in half. An' A'm not ganna tak' him in them clothes.'

When Tommy came back, he was carrying two complete suits and Johnnie was more than satisfied.

'Me Ma says ye'can 'av these cos A've grown oot o' them.'

Johnnie wasn't surprised. Tommy was going to be a big man. He was already a fair size for a boy of twelve. That was what had given Johnnie the idea. Tommy was as tall as their visitors.

Anyone who was walking the streets of Sandgate at the crack of dawn on that day would have seen them; an embarrassed Umberto being pushed along in a handcart by a giant of a man.

The only garment Umberto had willingly put on, was the strange blue bonnet that belonged to Johnnie. Several sizes too large of course. Johnnie thought that covering Umberto's 'funny haircut' would help to conceal his strange appearance. Umberto's reason for wearing the hat was quite different. A Roman soldier must surely hide his face in such situations. It was important to have his leg attended to, so he resigned himself that this was the way. All the same, in all his centuries of travel, he had never been required to wear such ridiculous clothes. How he wished that he could think of a password to send him back through time and space to Corbridge. He was sure that someone was trying to get him back along with Sam and that that was why they were moving forwards and backwards.

When he thought of Sam, he wondered why they had got into this situation in the first place. Way back in his memory was the thought that it had all begun with a game of chance. Sam had been a civilian worker at the fort at Vindolanda, Umberto a soldier in the great Roman Army. Umberto remembered how some fresh soldiers had engaged them in a game involving hypnosis. Before they knew what was happening, they were both charging along with hundreds of men, using bows and arrows. These weapons were absolutely new to Umberto. To Sam any weapon was new.

As a result, when he used it, the arrow flew where it pleased and some poor man got it in the eye. This resulted in a lot of cheering on the battlefield. Neither of the men knew why. They remained unaware that Sam's faltering shot had changed the course of history.

Somewhere, someone else was trying leave their mark on the pages of history and Sam and Umberto were whisked away to a ship on the high seas. There they were alarmed by the noise of firing canons. Since then, they had travelled backwards and forwards through decades and centuries. They had discovered America one day and seen New York growing skyscrapers, another. They had been on an expedition to The North Pole, then they had been washed up on the shore of a tropical island. Umberto's thoughts were dwelling happily on the glimpse of elegant limbs through the skirts of the dancing ladies when, sadly, they were interrupted. Johnnie hoisted him onto his shoulder and carried him up the steps of The Keelmen's Hospital. He then deposited Umberto on a bench and went off in search of help. How it was secured, is a mystery, but Umberto waited patiently.

Benny Weston was the bonesetter. 'Aw,' he said when he examined Umberto's leg, 'That'll not tak' lang.' Benny had a reputation of being able to cure some things in minutes. When he lifted Umberto's foot, the soldier winced. Whatever Benny did next, Umberto passed out with pain. When he surfaced and found that he could stand upright, he clasped the poor unprepared Benny by the shoulders and slapped a kiss on both cheeks. Embarrassment flooded Benny's face.

'Tak 'm away. Tak' 'm away.' Benny's voice followed them as they left.

Initially, Umberto objected to being carried down the steps and to once more, riding in the handcart. In view of the embarrassing suit he was wearing, he relented and agreed. When Johnnie explained that he needed to rest his foot for a while, Umberto was quite pleased with himself, that he understood. He began to practice the local tongue. That would surely impress Sam. The amused Johnnie could hear him muttering as they went along.

'Tak' 'm awy. Tak' 'm away.'

Johnnie wasn't nearly so amused when he arrived back at the keel to find Bobby Simpson there, reporting that Charlie, one of Johnnie's crew was sick and wouldn't be coming to work that day.

'What's ganen' on here?' Bobby asked, obviously referring to the unexpected company.

'Aw, there's no time ter tell yer now. We'll have ter be gannen. An' it looks as if he'll ha 'ter double up fer Charlie,' he said referring to Sam.

The day went well. Sam thought he'd never needed to work so hard but he enjoyed Johnnie's company and they entertained one another with tales of their individual experiences.

For several generations, Johnnie's family had been keelmen. Over the years some of them had been pressed into service and stories about their deeds, heroic and not so heroic had been handed down. There had been some hard times for them in the past, including strikes and poverty. There had been a time when some of their number had gathered on Newcastle Town Moor and spoken out in favour of 'Our King over the water.' Such treason had almost resulted in a hanging.

Johnnie offered to share his food with his two visitors but they declined. He refrained from offering his beer. A typical keelman, Johnnie liked his beer in large amounts. Slowly, he drank half of the amount he had brought along, allowing it to soothe the burning in his throat where the flying coal dust had settled. The drunkenness amongst the keelmen, was, no doubt, brought about as a direct result of the nature of their work.

Johnnie ate slices of bread which he cut from his large loaf, topping each with a slice of meat from the joint from his basket. He was almost finished his snack when Cuddy Armstrong came alongside.

'Whoa,' he called. 'Last one there's a cissie'

This, it seemed to Sam was an indication to work even harder to get the keel past the rest. He began to row with even greater vigour. Then, Sam thought it might help, if he used some of the phrases the keelmen used.

Echoing the voice of the rival keelman he called out, 'Wohoa there. Last a...'

Johnnie didn't hear him say another word. When he looked round both Sam and Umberto had disappeared. Johnnie's jaw dropped in disbelief. His eyes searched the keel and then he peered into the shallow water, but they weren't there. He couldn't see them in the huddock, but feeling the need to sit down, he occupied the small space himself, to reflect on what had happened. He could barely believe it. Johnnie shook his head, wondering what Gerty, his wife, would make of this strange tale.

But Gerty didn't believe a word of it.

The forerunner of the Royal National Lifeboat Institution was founded in Newcastle in 1790 with the name of Tyne Lifeboat Society. Its purpose was to offer a prize for the design of a boat which would remain upright and floating in the heaviest of seas. In the previous year the sailing ship 'Adventure' foundered on a sand bank in the mouth of the Tyne, with the loss of all her crew.

THE HUNGRY SEA
John Gamblin

'They will have their salt, whatever you visit upon me', shouted Jeremiah Beeching, threatening the heavens with a clenched fist and trying to avoid the sulphurous smoke. It pursued him incessantly, as if the gusting, on-shore wind could see every movement he made.

His frustration had begun with the impossible task of starting a fire under his salt pan. The force of the wind arriving at the mouth of the Tyne, unhindered by land, had driven him to find a leeward spot, in order to produce a shovelful of blazing coals. His return trek had been a painful one of scorched hands, singed clothing and profanity which would have earned him a ringing ear, had his Mother heard it. Finally his brazier was blazing, slowly evaporating the brine to leave a welcome ring of salt clinging to the side of his pan.

Though barely twenty, the North-easterner was already hardened to the effect of the unremitting wind lashing his coastline and so, was able to appreciate the relative comfort of the September sun. He climbed to the Law Top and stood on the edge, enjoying the sensations he had known since childhood. He felt the wind tugging and tearing at his clothing. He listened to the ceaseless beat of surf on sand. He watched kittiwakes cruising only inches above white-capped waves. He smelt the air, sharpened by the salt of the sea with which he survived. He marvelled at the effect of the Herd Sands, even on seas as huge as today's. The surface bubbled as vigorously as his boiling brine-pan and breakers crashed and smashed themselves on the underwater mountain.

He lifted his eyes from the ferocious pounding, to watch a two masted brig running before the wind. 'She should shorten sail', his instinct told him, 'if she intends coming in'. Despite the distance, he could sense the urgent straining of the deckhands to achieve that end. The ship rose and dipped, heeling all the while, in a sea coming at the vessel from all directions. Suddenly, with a flapping crack that could be heard, even above the furious gale, one corner of the mainsail broke away from its yard. The vessel veered sharply, catching Jacob Wooler, helmsman and master, totally unprepared. He lost his footing as the unmanned wheel became a revolving blur. The force which had been driving the brig forward, now attacked her from the side, challenging the recovered Wooler into an unequal struggle to bring the vessel into the wind once again. Agonisingly slowly the prow came around, revealing to the mariner's anxious eyes the turmoil of the Herd Sands. Too close to be avoided, the brig 'Adventure' was driven to a shuddering halt on the sand bank, broadside on to the relentless sea.

A mile or so away, the gale was stripping leaves from the trees in South Shields market place. Scurrying in rotating spheres, they searched for open doorways, sheltered corners, any windbreak where they could find rest. A breathless man scraped them aside in the lobby of St. Hilda's church, in order to open the door and rush to the office of the Parish Clerk. An invitation to enter answered his knock. William Wouldhave, known to his acquaintances as Willie, looked at the newcomer over the top of a high desk and raised a questioning eyebrow.

'I'm looking for the Vicar, Sir,' the man explained.

'I'm afraid he is not here at the moment. Can I be of assistance?'

'I don't think so, Sir. I was told first to get a doctor but then the Constable said, a doctor could do those men no good, better get a vicar.'

'You're not making a lot of sense, man', said Wouldhave, 'which men are you talking about?'

'The men on the boat, Sir. There's a brig aground on the Sands.'

'Well, I don't see what the Vicar can do about that. He's not a seaman, y' know.'

'Seamen can't do nothing neither, Sir. Sea's running high and fast. There's two o' them gone already. Swept off the deck like straws, Sir. 'N she's starting to break up.'

The clerk jumped to his feet. His chair toppled and clattered on the stone floor. 'I still don't know what the Vicar can do, but you're right. He should be told. You go about your business and I'll do the rest.'

Failing to locate the Vicar, Wouldhave left messages in several likely places and walked to see the incident for himself. Several hundred people had the same idea as he, but had had it considerably earlier. The Law Top was a seething mass of humanity, all well wrapped against the predatory wind. William quickly realised that his coat, though fashionable, was not practical against the rigours of such weather. Nevertheless, the drama held a grim fascination which he, like many others, could not resist. Steeling himself against the chill, he finally found a vantage point by scrambling onto a high rock. On the North side of the river, the swell of spectators swayed across any surface which afforded a view and William could clearly see figures clinging to the Priory ruins. As he settled himself a roar went up from those who had sight of the disaster.

'There's another gone.'
'He's in the water.'
'There he's come up again.'
'Is he swimming?'
'No. He's gone under.'
'That makes five.'
'It's only a matter of time for the rest of them.'
'They must be frozen. Soaking wet, and in this wind.'

Wouldhave detected despair and a sense of frustration in the voices. He could see the figures of several seamen, standing in the rigging, holding onto spars and ropes. He could only try to imagine the terror with which they viewed every enormous wave. Each time one broke across her, the stricken vessel disappeared behind an eruption of water and spray. The sails, now tasselled, slapped and cracked in a soaking frenzy. At that moment another fatigued seaman lost his grip. As he fell, the rope with which he had tried to secure himself, caught him around the neck. He swung from the yard arm with a nearby shipmate vainly reaching for him. William saw the sea as a greedy and cruel animal, devouring whatever it could reach, smashing its victims into easily digested pieces. Increasingly, what he watched, turned the frustration of helplessness into anger.

At the water's edge he heard a commotion erupt.

'Don't be bloody stupid, man', said one voice.

'Let go! I've got to try,' shouted another.

'You'll never get past the first breaker.'

'Give us a hand to push this through, then. I can't stand and watch.'

'You'll drown along with them. There's not a row boat made that could weather those seas.'

'I'm going.'

Two minutes later, Wouldhave heard a jumble of warnings, a crash and splintering wood.

'I warned you, you wouldn't get past the first breaker.'

The 'Adventure' rocked under another wave and when the spray disappeared, so had the seaman who had been hanging, as well as the rigging and the shipmate who had tried to release him.

Sickened, William returned to his work at St. Hilda's. As he turned towards his office he caught sight of the crucifix, hanging over the altar. He stood and looked at it, shaking his head as the words of the man at the water's edge rang through his brain. 'There's not a row boat made that could weather those seas.'

Legend has it that William Wouldhave got the idea for the design of an unsinkable boat while watching a walnut shell floating in his bath and that Henry Greathead merely modified it. However, Greathead was awarded the cash prize!

19TH CENTURY

Under Elvet Bridge is part of the Chapel of St. James, which became a Correction House. One internee was Jimmy Allan, the Gypsy Piper, who, in 1803 was sentenced to hang for stealing a horse. The sentence was commuted to life imprisonment and the Piper served seven years, dying a few days before his pardon came through. Some say you can still hear his pipes.

THE GHOST PIPER
Sandra Salmon

Notes hang in the air, soft as autumn smoke,
Drifting down the years.
My footsteps ring hollow,
Tippy tap, tippy tap.
I should not have walked this path alone
But the music entices me on.

'He's guilty,' they say,
'Hang the man.'
Tippy tap, tippy tap.
For taking a horse?
Tippy tap, tippy tap.
The music draws me on.

'Imprisonment then.
Take him to the Correction House.'
No! Music is freedom
And his pipes sing so true.
Tippy tap, tippy tap.
The music drives me on.

'A pardon! A mere seven years and a pardon.'
What use is it now?
Tippy tap, tippy tap.
Notes shatter in my head,
Plummeting down the years.
The music skirls to silence.

Although steam powered transport had been used inside industrial sites for some years, it needed the scarcity of horses, caused by the demands of the Napoleonic wars, to animate entrepreneurs, such as Edward Pease, to seek cheaper ways of transporting their coal from the pit-head to the factory. The first steam engine to haul both passengers and goods started from Shildon in County Durham on 27th September 1825. Unfortunately, the first striking match was not invented until 1826.

THE TRAIN NOW STANDING
John Gamblin

'Haad them gallowa's steady theor.'

The ear punishing dialect of the unloading crew carried above the thump of straining hooves, the persuasive babble of assorted vendors and the muttering undertow from several hundred South Durhamites, pulled to the occasion by curiosity.

'Dus they Newcassel chaps spake English, thinks tha, Mr. Potts?'

'They migh' Mr. Chambers, leastway unnerstan-a-bit-on't.'

In deference to what the 'Durham Advertiser' had insisted would be an historic occasion, these two had dressed in their 'going to market' clothes. Pristine leather gaiters connected corduroy breeches to highly polished brown boots. Tweed jackets, worn unbuttoned, revealed moleskin waistcoats. Potts, toweringly eminent at six feet three, wore a black three-cornered hat which normally saw only Sunday daylight, while his friend favoured a brimmed felt hat, more closely related to the weathering his face had endured.

'Yon wa'int come off that wagon looks tha.'

'Yon' was an iron object, rotund and black, with an elephantine snout pointing skywards. Its horse-drawn journey through the narrow lanes from Newcastle to Shildon had created interest, enough to concoct a carnival atmosphere for the crowd who jostled along with Potts and Chambers. At that moment, 'yon' was being coaxed from its platform onto a new habitat of parallel iron strips.

'Haad yer hosses still, Tucker, till wa hev the ramp fast.'

Potts and Chambers shrugged shoulders, totally perplexed,

while four big iron wheels endured Tynesider's shouts and curses. Four straining horses controlled the machine's descent of the ramp.

'Yon's hot work today I'm thinking, Mr. Chambers.'

'Yon's hot work any day, Mr. Potts, but today 'specially. It's too hot by half for September. We'll pay for it later looks tha, mark me words.'

'Mebbe so, but later's later. We should only worry 'bout right now. Right now what do you say to a flagon of ale?'

'Well, Mr. Potts, my immediate inclination is to say yes, but - having come so far and waited so long - I don't want to miss seeing this contraption move.'

'Think on't, Mr. Chambers. Ted Pease isn't due for two hours yet. It's not going to move afore him is't?'

Ten minutes later the pair discovered that many others had conceived the same idea as they coughed their way through a cloud of tobacco smoke to the bar of the 'George Inn' at Heighington. It took a further five minutes before they found the shade of an oak tree, ale foaming down the sides of earthenware mugs and over their fingers. A fellow seeker of shade had already seated himself with his back against the furrowed trunk.

'Morning, Gents.'

The pair returned the compliment affably, before settling themselves around the tree. Their companion busied himself with a knife, his big hands cutting delicate slivers from a block of black tobacco. His rough wool trousers had the bottoms held clear of the ground by lengths of twine, knotted immediately below the knees, as if he had only just arrived from a bout of manual labour. The narrow blue stripe of his collarless flannelette shirt did not diminish the breadth of his shoulders nor the bulge of his biceps. The bowl of the clay pipe gripped between his teeth had acquired the same chocolate colour as the sun had given his face. As if to emphasise the pipe's emptiness he sucked on it from time to time, making a sound like an emptying drain.

'Exciting day, eh?' The curiosity of Edwin Potts cracked first.

The man took his pipe by the bowl and with a flick of the wrist, sent a streamer of gunk from the mouthpiece to trace a glistening track across grass and moss.

'Aye, for some mebbe,' he replied, carefully rubbing the tobacco into his pipe.

'Not for you then, Sir, it seems.'

'Matters not one way or t'other. I've seen enough of that wagonway over the last couple of years not to be excited with it.'

'So! You worked on it then, Mister ... ?'

The workman smiled, paused and said, 'Metcalfe. Aye, I worked on it and now it's finished.'

'What will you do now then, Mr. Metcalfe?' Joseph Chambers joined the conversation.

'Who knows? There's always work if you're willing.'

The pipe filled to his satisfaction he stood and walked into the sun's glare. From his pocket he removed a reading glass and manoeuvred sun, glass and pipe bowl into a line as straight as the tobacco juices drying on the nearby grass. Smoke quickly issued from the tiny spot of concentrated sunlight and Metcalfe expertly puffed it into life before resettling himself.

'By, yon's a smart trick,' congratulated Chambers, 'but what happens if it's raining?'

'Aa saves a good bit on me baccer,' replied the smoker, a contented grin splitting his face.

The two friends stayed a while longer than their new acquaintance and, as they returned to the event with a further quart and a half of ale swilling around the stomach of each, a carriage, drawn by a glistening black stallion, passed them. The single passenger wore the wide brimmed black hat, favoured by the Society of Friends.

'That's Teddy Pease, Mr. Potts. Just arriving - Halloa Teddy. Best of luck...' The carriage passenger turned in his seat, gave one hard look and turned once again to face forward.

'That was Teddy Pease, Mr. Potts. I'd know him anywhere.'

His companion roared with laughter. 'He'll know you, Mr. Chambers, the next time he claps eyes on you. Ha Ha. Come on or we'll miss it all.' And still laughing he walked on.

'Might I have a minute, Mr. Potts?'

With what dignity survived Potts' ribaldry and his own intentions, he walked into the undergrowth, treading bramble underfoot. His left shoulder lent support to an ancient elm tree while his right hand fumbled with his breeches buttons.

'Go steady, Mr. Chambers that cost threepence ha'penny a quart.' and his laughter ended with a loud hiccup.

Eventually they arrived at the main celebration in time to hear a man in a high top hat and black frock coat inviting the assembly to welcome Mr. Edward Pease.

'Thank you, Mr. Stephenson. Welcome ladies and gentlemen to this historic event on this fine day ...'

'Its your friend, Mr. Chambers. You know - Teddy,' reported Potts, as loud as a tree full of crows.

'I can't see', complained his diminutive friend.

'You don't need to. Just listen.'

And listen they did; to the history of the undertaking; to the skill of the engineer; to the industry of the work force; to the hopes for the future. The only interruption came as Chambers passed his silver hip flask to Potts. Chambers was particularly fond of Jamaica rum, only partly because it released any excess of wind he might have. The resultant belch emerged from the deepest regions of the little man who, in turn, was delighted to have Edwin Potts standing head and shoulders over him, holding a flask of alcohol. Potts himself adopted an innocent face in the hope that it would divert the speaker's wrath.

'... and so ladies and gentlemen, back to Mr. Stephenson and his machine, so aptly named "Locomotion". The machine, like a living thing, has been fed and watered, and now needs only the addition of energy to transport us at a breathtaking fifteen miles an hour. Mr. Stephenson, that is your honour, Sir.'

'If we had been meant to move at fifteen miles an hour we'd have been given four legs instead of two,' murmured a less than gruntled Edwin Potts. Meanwhile, Chambers, in an attempt to cure the slurring which he would, if questioned, attribute to the unseasonable heat, was manufacturing another belch. That accomplished he addressed his companion:

'Agh, the choleric face doesn't suit you, Mr. Potts. You'll feel better when we're in one o' them wagons.'

'One o' them wagons? Ye're not gettin me in one o' they. Anyway, we're not invited. Ho, but wait! Mayhap Teddy sent you a personal invite to go wi'im, wha?'

But at that very moment it became clear that no one was going anywhere. Edward Pease, with bowed head, listened to the whispered tones of George Stephenson. Fluttering hands and shaking heads revealed their agitation. Finally, Pease angrily gestured at the rostrum and Stephenson took his place on it.

'Ladies and gentlemen,' George Stephenson raised his voice

above the buzz of anticipation, 'Mr. Pease and his Company apologise for the delay, which perhaps some kind person among you may be able to remedy.' He gave his words several seconds to be digested. 'As you will know "Locomotion" relies on steam power and to create steam we must light the boiler.' Stephenson paused once more. 'To make the spark we normally carry a flint and steel in the tool kit but, on this occasion, this appears to have been overlooked. Does one among you carry such an item on their person?'

The shocked silence lasted fifteen seconds, breaking to a low murmur, growing to a groan of incredulous surprise. Catcalls, whistles, guffaws and less than complimentary remarks came from all parts of the gallery - but no flint and steel. Stephenson raised a hand. 'A man has been sent to Aycliffe for a lantern. I crave your indulgence. Thank you.'

Edwin Potts removed a hand from his pocket and opened it to the flickering gaze of his compatriot, whose eyes eventually focussed on a flint and steel.

'Lend it to them, Mr. Potts.'

'I don't think so, Mr. Chambers. That's how the likes of your friend Teddy get rich, by not buying flints and steels and such.' And closed the discussion with a hiccup.

In the front rank of the spectators a man stood, looking thoughtful. A stained clay pipe jutted from his sun darkened face while his knife pared thin slivers from a block of black tobacco. He closed the knife and, putting it and the tobacco into the pocket of his flannelette shirt, he strolled towards the group of engineers, waiting anxiously at the side of 'Locomotion'.

'Mr. Stephenson, Sir,' he said, offering his magnifying glass, 'I think this might be the answer to your problem.'

In October 1831 the first case of Asiatic cholera was reported in Sunderland and it quickly spread from there to Newcastle and Gateshead and through the country. In Newburn out of 550 inhabitants 424 people became ill, of whom 57 died. Amongst them was the vicar, the Rev. James Edmonson. The Rev. John Reed was appointed two months later. At the time of this story it was not known that the cause of the cholera was polluted drinking water. The appearance of this disease led to rapid action to improve living conditions of the poor.

THE VICAR OF NEWBURN
Eve Stockmann

For a long time, until quite recently, I resented James Edmonson - more so because we once had been very close friends. I stopped myself thinking about him, I wanted nothing more to do with him and a few months ago I would never have believed that I would be standing here now.

I remember the first day we met at Oxford. One morning I was late for my class and ran down a corridor, when suddenly the door next to me opened and someone, balancing what seemed like a tower of books, stepped out of that room and we collided, the tower disintegrating into a clatter.

'You should watch were you are going,' I shouted angrily, my headache, the result of the previous night's wine party, responding to the commotion.

'I know,' was all he said and at the same time he smiled in a manner which, I thought, my sisters would have called disarming or sweet and even I could not stay angry any longer.

We both laughed at the litter of books on the floor and while we were picking them up, we discovered that we were both attending the same class.

James could hardly ever be persuaded to go rowing boats or to join wine parties, nothing mattered to him more than to excel in his studies. But he also made friends easily and had a way of making people feel important which made him one of the most popular students in Oxford. And when he became a member of the debating society, he also became one of the most talked about.

He was a brilliant speaker and defended his ideals with an

intensity which was new to us. His father had died when James was only five and had left very little to his widow and child. If it hadn't been for his bachelor uncle, James would never have had the means to attend university. This is how he sympathised more with the poor than the rest of us, who had enjoyed more comfortable lives, and he was ceaselessly trying to stir our consciences.

Once, after a visit to his uncle's, who lived near Middlesbrough, James became very angry when someone - I think it was Joe Henderson - complained about the sort of people who were flocking to the fast growing new towns, of which Middlesbrough was one.

'Who else would want to work at these ironworks than the people you call rough? What would you be like if you had to travel the country for work, if you had no permanent roof over your head and if you had no education?'

'All right, all right.' Joe realised that he had gone a little too far and tried to adopt a conciliatory tone. 'If that's the case, they should all be happy about the houses they are getting, near to their work. But not all of them are.'

'Have you ever been in one of them?'

'No. Have you?'

'No, but my uncle has. He says they are damp and that it is quite common for nine people to live in one room.'

'Yes, and their pigs ... ' someone interjected and everybody laughed apart from the two antagonists. By now Joe was determined not to lose his argument, the way he usually did.

'What do you expect? The houses must be built as quickly as possible and they must be cheap. That's why they must be no bigger than absolutely necessary.'

'They are obviously not big enough. Nine people to a room, I ask you. Some people even brick their windows up in order not to pay window tax! Can you imagine the stench in some of those houses? We praise the miracles of civilisation, but in these places civilized man is turned back almost into a savage. Can you imagine a better breeding ground for disease? I dread to think of what would happen if we ever got the plague back again!'

He said that ten years ago! If only ...

At the time we thought, me included, that he was exaggerating and that his vision lacked practicality. Instead we tried to convince him that, after all, work was the main necessity for these people. I still hear Joe finishing this argument with, 'it would be lunacy to waste money on anything which merely improves sanitary conditions,' and I still see the sad, resigned look on James' face.

As time went on he became increasingly convinced that the poor needed someone to speak up for them and that this someone had to be him. I distanced myself more and more from James' views because I considered them to be too radical. I often agreed with him in theory, of course, but I felt that in order to cope with every day life, one had to make concessions. After all, we had to earn a living once we left Oxford and, in my opinion, a curate who concerned himself more with the interpretation of the scriptures than with high minded political ideas had a better chance of advancement.

James was a frequent visitor in my parents' house and became like a second brother to my sisters. Elizabeth may have had more than sisterly feelings for him once but I think James was completely unaware of that. Besides, Elizabeth knew very well that both my father and I considered him to be an unsuitable match for anyone, as long as his reformist ideas could get in the way of a stable position in the church. And then, of course, there was my cousin Eleanor whom I had adored ever since I can remember.

She came for a visit one summer when James was staying with us and soon they had only eyes for each other. They both confided in me, thinking that I was the one who could share their feelings best because I knew them both so well. Eleanor would praise James' wit, his intelligence, his care and engagement for others and even thought he was good looking. Whatever else James was, good looking he was not. Strangely enough, it never seemed to matter to the ladies. They never complained about him being too thin and too tall, nor did they ever seem to notice how he constantly had to sweep a strand of his straight hair away from his eyes, a habit which I found irritating.

For James it was the first time that he was in love, and my jealousy grew with each of his monologues on the beauty and virtues of Eleanor. And yet, I could not stop myself listening to him. He expressed everything I had ever felt for her so beautifully, but it hurt to think that he was describing his own feelings and not mine. For a while I was hoping that their attraction for each other might wane, that James' demanding idealism would be too much for Eleanor who had had a very protective upbringing, but instead she rose to the challenge and became as determined as him to do whatever she could do to relieve the plight of the poor.

I can't remember those weeks very well. All I remember is the torment I felt because the friend whom I admired and respected had betrayed me, in taking away from me the only person whom I had ever wanted to become my wife. Maybe I had never said that in so many words, but he knew me so well, he should have understood. And also, how could he be so irresponsible as to expect a woman to share the life he had chosen for himself, that of a political activist?

James was, I think, oblivious to what was going on inside my head and was genuinely taken aback when, in the way of conversation, I told him that he had to moderate the way in which he was expressing his views.

'What are you saying? They are not only my views. We both agree, don't we, that much has to be done to help the poor?'

'Yes, yes, of course.'

'And you also agree, don't you, that it is our duty as ministers of the Church to put their case to those who have enough influence.'

'Yes, of course. I know that we can do it better than the poor people themselves, but not the way you are doing it. At the moment the Archdeacon fears - so I heard say - that you might use your sermons to stir up unrest among the lower orders.'

The colour drained out of James' cheeks and his eyes searched my face in vain for a sign that I did not mean what I was saying.

'Nonsense, you are making this up.'

'Why don't you go and ask the Archdeacon yourself?'

Anger rushed colour back into James' face. 'Why don't you admit, John, that this has nothing to do with my convictions. This is because of Eleanor. You are in love with her, but she doesn't love you, she loves me!'

At that moment I wished him dead.

I only understood much later that James felt betrayed by me, too. If I had stood by him, he thought, others would have supported us, but without me … ? I don't think he knew before that I was not prepared to take risks which threatened my livelihood. From then on he never failed to comment on it with bitter disdain, whenever the occasion arose. At the same time, though, he modified his behaviour and did all he could to dispel the notion that he could not be entrusted with a parish.

In preparation for her marriage to James, Eleanor started teaching at a Sunday School and she wrote excited letters to my sisters, praising this new institution which gave working class children a chance of some education, imagining how that might affect their future lives. I don't think she ever thought that working there might shorten her life. One of the children had apparently been feeling ill for a day or two but did not want to miss school. After a few days Eleanor became ill with a fever and died a week later. For a long time I could not think of her without blaming James: because of him she disregarded the comfort and security she had always known and that had cost her her life.

Some time later Joe Henderson told me that James had become vicar at Newburn. 'Just the right place for him,' he laughed. 'Most of the inhabitants are very poor.'

Our lives would probably never have touched again if the region had not been visited by this dreadful cholera which now has been raging for over four months.

John Whitfield was the first one to mention it to me. 'Have you read about these deaths in Sunderland?'

'You mean the old keelman and his son?'

'Yes, and the old nurse at the infirmary who helped to put the son's body in the coffin. And the son's little girl.'

'But she didn't die.'

'All the same, the doctors say it's highly contagious.'

'Others believe that it's not.'

'So, do you think it's cholera?'

'Well, it's too early to tell. The sanitary conditions in the towns are so much better than they were two hundred years ago ... '

'You wouldn't say that if you lived in Bailiffgate or Backrow.'

'I don't know that area very well. But this William Sproat, the keelman, lived in a large, clean, well ventilated room. It may just be a common bowel complaint, the sort which visits every town in the country every autumn.'

I did not want to believe that it was the cholera. I did not want to think of dirt, squalor and disease. I did not want James to be right.

But I could not close my eyes for long to what was going on around me. Hundreds died in the region and, as James had predicted, it affected mainly the lower orders. The local authorities took a sudden interest in ill-ventilated and dirty places in the towns where infection could be spread rapidly and recommended the interiors of such houses to be washed with hot lime, at the expense of the owners or their tenants! Many tenants could not pay, many owners, at first, did not want to. John Whitfield told me that at the height of the outbreak bells tolled constantly from the various churches in Newcastle and Gateshead. It must have been a mournful sight: the seemingly endless number of corpses being transported through the streets, many of them without a single attendant.

In Ryton, my former parish, we were discussing ways to check the progress of the disease and it was suggested to buy such as blankets, clogs, stockings, shirts and trousers for the poor. By Christmas we were still only halfhearted in our attempts. Even though it spread rapidly, many people believed that the cholera would only ravage in the big towns. I don't think anybody believed that a village like Newburn could suffer such dreadful devastation. Almost every house here must have been visited by the cholera, three quarters of the population were ill! And one tenth died. One of them was James.

On first hearing of his death, I felt no more sorrow for him than for all the others who had fallen victim to this pestilence. Then I was taken over by resentment. He had gone and by doing so he had betrayed me again. Betrayed me? Yes, I needed him to forgive me and he was not there. Now I wanted to explain myself, now I wanted to say the things I had left unsaid before, but now he was not there.

I wanted to make amends for my failures, and the only way I knew how to do that, was by visiting Newburn.

I asked for the key to the church at the grave diggers house. 'Are you wanting to be the new vicar?' he asked hopefully.

'No, no. I'm the Reverend John Reed from Ryton. Reverend Edmonson was a friend of mine. I don't know if it's possible to see his grave, but I would like to say a prayer for him in the church.'

'You better say one for all the others, too.'

'For all the others?'

'Surely, you must know.'

'Know what?'

'That after the death of Mr. Edmonson no funeral rites are being performed over those who die of the cholera.'

'No funeral rites?' I repeated mechanically while I was trying to shape my thoughts into cohesion. Could I stand back, waiting for someone willing to be the new vicar of Newburn, once the danger has passed? That could take a long time. The people here needed a vicar, now more than ever. What was it like for them, their loved ones having been buried without funeral rites? I knew how it hurt me, thinking of James.

The grave digger, taking my silence to be due to a lack of compassion, went on, 'The corpses are not allowed to enter the church and we can't find anyone willing to read the service over the graves. There's just me. All I can do for the dead is to throw some lime over their coffins and bury them.'

'But I can do more.' There was no doubt in my mind that I had made the right decision.

Here I am now, James, looking at the big window which carries your name. In about an hour I shall preach my first sermon as the new vicar of Newburn and then I will read the funeral service over your grave and those of the others. Perhaps it needed something like your death to shake me, and many others, out of our lethargy, but I shall try my utmost to make sure that it was not in vain.

A statue of Charles Stewart stands in the market square of Durham City. It was unveiled on 2nd December, 1861. He is most famous for the building of Seaham Harbour.

A MAN ON A HORSE
Tina O'Neill

It was almost midnight. Henry sat on his bed looking at the postcard he had received that morning. He had never received a postcard before. Next to his name and address was a short message. Henry read it aloud, it said: 'To my friend Henry. Hope you like the picture. Your mate Tom. P.S. I got a friend to write this for me.'

The picture on the other side was of a man on a horse in the market place of a city called Durham. What worried Henry more than anything was that he didn't know anyone called Tom.

The next morning, January the 12th, 1999, was Henry's eighth birthday and he received a computer from his parents. His father put it in Henry's bedroom. Henry had no idea what he wanted to do. Then he saw the postcard. His father had said, anybody who was anybody was on the Internet these days. Under the words 'Man on a Horse' it said: 'Charles Stewart, the third Marquess of Londonderry.' Henry opened up his Internet file and asked it to search for Charles Stewart. Soon he found himself looking at the postcard picture on his computer screen. There was lots of writing about the man on the horse. It said he owned collieries in Durham and that he had built a harbour in a place called Seaham. Henry wrote down a few notes and went off to find his father.

George Waybe was in the sitting room reading the paper. Henry could smell spices, jelly and pies.

'Mum's baking,' he said to no one in particular.

George Waybe looked up from his paper. He put his finger to his lips and said

'Shh, your Mam wants to surprise you, lad. Don't spoil it for her now. Come on, up to your room and I'll help you with your computer.'

Henry sat on the bed and his father on the chair in front of the computer.

'Have you found anything of interest yet?' he asked.
'I looked up my Man on the Horse.'
'Who?'
Henry picked up the postcard and gave it to his father.
'Who's Tom?'
'I don't know.'
'He sent you this card.'
'I know, but I don't know anyone called Tom. I liked the picture, though.'
'Well, who's the Man on the Horse then?' Henry told his father all about Charles Stewart.
'Would you like to see his statue, Henry?'
'For real, you mean?'
'Yes, for real. Your Mam's going to visit your Aunt Sarah tomorrow in Darlington. She's going on the train. Darlington is not far from Durham, so if we take her in the car, we could go into Durham and see your Man on the Horse. What do you say, lad?'
'Yes please, Dad. Can we?'
'I'll talk to your mother tonight. Not a word from you mind, until I've spoken to her. O.K.?' Henry agreed.
When his mother called them down for tea, he found his school friends, Jim and Carl, waiting for him at the bottom of the stairs.
'Party guests,' his father explained as they all entered the sitting room.
Henry was greatly relieved that his mother didn't expect them to play party games, but allowed them to go upstairs, to have a go on the computer. When Jim and Carl left at almost nine o'clock, Henry's father was in the sitting room, watching the TV.
'Have you asked yet, Dad?'
'Asked what?' came his mother's voice from the kitchen. Henry looked at the carpet and shuffled his feet.
'Your mother asked you a question, Henry?'
'We can go, can't we?'
'Go where, love?'
'To Durham, Mam, me Dad says we can.'
'Does he now, Henry?'
'Well, as good as.'
Mrs Waybe smiled at her son. 'Well, how can I refuse you, Henry? And besides, it does mean, I get to travel in comfort.'
'Hooray! I'm going to Durham.'

'Right now, Henry, you're going to bed.' Henry drifted off to sleep holding on to his postcard.

As he tried to turn over in his bed, he felt a hand grab hold of him. He opened his eyes and found himself looking at a young boy. Henry screamed and jumped up. He looked around. This was not his bedroom!

'Calm down, lad. I only held you, so as you wouldn't fall off and hurt your head.'

Henry turned and looked at the boy. His clothes were covered in dirt, his hair was short and his face was unwashed. He was sitting on a wooden bench outside a large building, the same bench as the one Henry had nearly fallen from.

'Who are you?'

'Tom's my name, lad. Pleased to meet you.' The boy held out his hand, and Henry shook it.

'How did I get here?'

'Can't say, lad. Last night I went to sleep on this bench, and when I woke there you were beside me. May I ask your name, lad?'

'My name's Henry. Could you tell me where we are, please?'

'Well, Henry, we're in Durham Market Square.'

Henry sat down on the bench and sobbed.

'Why, there be no need to cry, lad. Durham don't look that bad, does it?'

Henry sniffled and wiped his nose on the sleeve of his dirty shirt. 'Me Mam will kill me when she sees the state of me clothes.'

'What's wrong with your clothes, Henry?'

'Look at em, they're filthy.'

'They look fine to me, Henry, but I don't see too well. One too many good hidings from me Dad.'

'I didn't know, Tom. I'm sorry. Can you write, Tom?'

'Nay, lad, I can't write. Why do you ask?'

'I got a postcard from someone called Tom. I thought it might have been you.'

'What's a postcard, Henry?'

'It's like a letter, but it has a picture on one side.'

'What picture did yours have on?'

'It was a picture of that statue over there, in the middle of the square.'

'It was put up yesterday. There were lots of people about.

Don't know what all the fuss was about me self. Nobody round here liked the man. What's it look like, Henry, describe it to me.'

'It's a man on a horse. It's standing on a square stone with writing on. The horse looks as if it's trotting.'

'Is anybody watching us, Henry?'

'No, everybody seems to be so busy, except one man with a bag of tools. He's just standing looking at the statue.'

'Maybe he made it!'

'He's walking away now, but he's left his tools.'

'Take me to the statue and help me pick up the tools, Henry.'

'Why? The man might come looking for them.'

'If he does, Henry, he might give two honest lads a penny or two for looking after them, and if not, they might fetch a nice penny or two at the pawnshop. Either way, you and I might eat tonight.'

The pair made their way over to the statue. Henry picked up the tool bag and Tom felt around the statue. 'Feels smooth but cold to the hands. Henry, come and feel.'

Henry stood in silence and watched his new friend feeling his way around the statue.

'Henry, this here horse has problems. Can you hear me, Henry? This poor horse has no tongue.'

Henry came closer and looked. Tom was right. Henry opened the tool bag and found a chisel and a hammer.

'What you doing, Henry, lad?'

'Shh, Tom, this isn't easy you know. I've only ever seen it done on the telly.'

'Seen what done? And what's a telly?'

'You mean you've never heard of a television, Tom?'

'Nay, lad, I've not. Now what you doing?'

'All done, Tom.'

Tom felt inside the mouth. 'You made it a tongue, Henry.'

'Climb down, Tom. I've got an idea.' Henry led Tom to the front of the square stone. Here they found a plaque which said: Charles William Vane Stewart, The Third Marquess of Londonderry, 1861. By Ralph Monti.

Henry read the words to Tom then took out the little chisel and hammer and wrote underneath: WITH HELP FROM HENRY AND TOM. He rubbed dirt into the letters, so that no one could see it.

'But we'll know it's there, Henry, and any time I like, I can come and feel the letters.'

The two boys went back and sat on the bench.

'Are you hungry, Henry?'

'A little.'

'Come, we'll see if Mr Greenwell has anything for us.'

'Who's Mr Greenwell, Tom?'

'Do you not know anything, lad? He be the owner of the big shop on Silver Street. He sometimes puts his old bread and the like in his back yard. If you're quick, you can get a good feed.'

'What about the tools, Tom?'

'We'll hide them under the bench till we get back.'

Tom ran ahead and Henry reluctantly followed him. It wasn't far to the backyard of the shop. Tom ran inside and came out with a lump of stale bread and a piece of mouldy cheese. Before Henry could speak, he heard a whistle blow and Tom was running again, calling to him,

'Run, Henry. Run for your life!'

Henry caught up with Tom in the Market Square. He sat on the bench where they had first met and was eating the bread and cheese.

'I thought he must have got you, lad.'

'Who were we running from, Tom?'

'The law, Henry. They don't like us taking from the yard.'

'Mr Greenwell puts the food there for you, doesn't he?'

'Don't be silly, Henry. He puts it there cos he can't sell it.'

'You mean we stole that food?'

'How else can we feed ourselves, Henry? Here eat. It's good.'

Henry ate only a little. He was very hungry but it tasted so bad that he felt sick inside. Tom devoured everything. Then the two boys fell asleep on the bench.

Henry woke to a buzzing sound and opened first one eye, then the other. He was in his own bedroom. The postcard was on the floor. He ran along the hall and into his parents' room.

'I know who Tom is!'

'Come on, down stairs. I want to hear all about it.'

Henry followed his father, telling him all about Tom and their adventure.

When he had finished, his father sat at the kitchen table, smiling.

'Henry it was all a dream, son.'

'No, Dad, it was real. Tom is real.'

'Well, we'll see soon enough, lad. We want to make an early start, so when you've finished your breakfast you'd better hurry and dress.'

Henry never said a word all the way to Darlington.

At Aunt Sarah's he ate one ham sandwich. He couldn't bring himself to eat the cheese ones. He drank his orange juice and then asked his father if they could go.

'Henry, you've just got here.'

'I'm sorry, Mam, but I want to see the statue.'

Aunt Sarah asked, 'What statue?' While Dad explained, Henry sat fidgeting on his chair. Aunt Sarah laughed.

Henry kissed his Aunt and ran to the car. He sat in silence once more as his father drove him to Durham. He followed him out of the car park and across a bridge, up a cobbled street with shops on either side. Henry walked slower and slower up the street.

'What's wrong, Henry?'

'I don't remember any of this.'

When they reached the top of the street, Henry saw many people walking around market stalls. Behind the stalls he could see the statue.

'Look, Dad, the bench!'

George Waybe looked at the bench, then at his son.

Henry bent down to look at the plaque on the base of the statue. He had to brush away lots of mud and dust, but underneath it all was the name of the statue maker, and written below were the words: WITH HELP FROM HENRY AND TOM.

In the early 1850s two pits were sunk in Seaham, the High Pit by the Hetton Coal Company, and the Low Pit by the Londonderry family. It is generally accepted that they shared the nickname with a local publican, Tommy Chilton, whose hobby was creating and selling nick-nacks. In its early years the 'Nicky-Nack' was notorious for loss of life. This was partly due to the fact that the two shafts of the High and Low pits were not connected. Despite rectifying this in 1862, one hundred and sixty four men and boys and one hundred and eighty one ponies died when a massive explosion tore through the pit on 8th September, 1880.

THE NICKY-NACK
David Cummings

It was in the eighteen fifties,
When they sunk the Nicky-Nack.
With dust to clog the lungs up,
And stone, to break the back.

She was a fire-breathing demon,
Who took so many lives.
She started in her first six weeks,
And six poor souls had died.

The youngest of them, only ten,
As firedamp snuffed them out.
A naked light was what they blamed.
Of that, there was no doubt.

Though toil and work went on and on,
Her temper rose again.
They heard the blast, and caught the flash.
And twenty-one were slain.

For many months, the pit stayed closed,
And no one worked the coal.
Until once more, we journeyed deep
Inside her vicious soul.

Again, she found within herself
The hate to take more lives.
One hundred sixty four would never
See mothers, nor their wives.

'Take my life, for what it's worth.
Take me now,' I said.
She must have taken pity then,
I was burnt, but wasn't dead.

Though death, lay all around me.
Scattered, men and boys,
I saw the light from someone's lamp.
I heard my saviour's voice.

So many perished on that night,
Survivors, there were few.
I thank the Lord that I was saved
To bring this tale to you.

This story is inspired by the many accidents which have occurred throughout the coalfields of Durham.

THE PRICE OF COAL
Ron Gray

The shotfirer sat on a wood chock and rested his back against a six-foot prop. Foreshift was a dreaded shift. Frank was getting on in years and crawling along a two feet high coal face at three o'clock in the morning did not suit him anymore. While sitting, he prodded holes into sticks of explosive to receive the tiny detonators. Then, he stuffed them into a crude toolbox, made from a piece of conveyor belt, with all his other bits and pieces. He called out to the other five miners, 'Ah'll be fire'n a few shots in the Mothergate, so dinna let anybody past ya!'

He took a deep breath and with some effort threw his gear before him, down the hundred yard face. A final adjustment to his kneepads, then he ducked under the caunch and followed his toolbox.

The other miners hardly noticed him as his cap lamp was swallowed up by the inky blackness. Tom stopped shovelling the pile of stone in order to adjust his battery to a more comfortable position round his waist. He pulled a filthy handkerchief from his pocket and wiped his brow, 'What was he on aboot before? Did he mention gas? He's gett'n like a bloody ard woman!'

Arthur, one of the others, looked up, 'He said the gas was up, but when he checked again, it was OK.'

Tom shrugged, attacked the pile of stone again and thought about the pork sandwiches in his haversack and the broken window in his greenhouse. Just as he was about to throw a shovelful of stone behind him, he froze at the sound of a muffled crack which came from far down the face. Fine, powder-like dust was dislodged from the timber supports and slowly descended through the light of his cap lamp.

The others stopped working. Only their eyes moved. Full shovels were gently lowered on to the stone floor. Picks were laid down. On their hands and knees they resembled a herd of nervous gazelles. Only the rivulets of sweat, snaking down their glistening bodies, were moving. One of them broke the silence by asking Tom if anything was wrong.

'Nowt wrong, ah just thought it sounded like a stone shot. Funny, them fire'n a stone shot though. Ah mean, they haven't had time to drill a bloody hole!'

Not waiting for a response, Tom dipped under the overhang of stone and started to make his way down the face. About fifty yards in, he began to feel a little uneasy. He should have heard the other team of miners working in the Mothergate, instead there was an eerie silence. Another couple of yards and he noticed a wave of thick, yellow smoke inching towards him. He strained his eyes, trying to see through it. It was almost upon him when he saw a faint glow. He shouted, 'Who's there? Is that you, Frank?'

'Aye, it's me, Tom. For God's sake, help me!'

Tom took a deep breath and plunged through the smoke. He found Frank gasping for breath, 'Ah fired a shot and there was an explosion. The whole bloody lot went up. Tell the lads to get out.'

Without a word, Tom turned Frank on his back and quickly loosened his shirt buttons. He then bunched Frank's coat collar into his fist and started to drag the shotfirer away from the smoke, all the time screaming for the others to help.

'Get ya arses doon here and give's a hand!'

Frank gripped Tom's arm, 'When Ah fired the shot the bloody lot went up. Ah shouted to the others, but there was no answer.'

More miners arrived quickly on the scene, their cap lamps picking out the two men, and soon they were in the comparative safety of the Tailgate. The wall of smoke was still creeping up the face. There was little time.

Tom stared at the floor, while the others started to blurt out suggestions on what to do. He searched the map in his brain, the map of the labyrinth of tunnels which had been dug out over the hundred and fifty years the pit had been open. He had been there the longest out of the group and knew the mine like his back yard. He also knew that any decision they made at that moment had to be the right one.

'Shush, man! Dinna panic, or we'll get neewhere. Now look, there must be a blockage because the wind's stopped. We canna gan doon the face because of the obvious, so grab ya coats and watter bottles and mak yer way down the Tailgate. We'll tak spells carry'n Frank. One of ya hang on to 'is lamp for a spare.'

At first, despite the foul air, they made good progress. The Tailgate was long and had been neglected over the years. It was not so bad when walking normally but trying to carry a fourteen stone man was proving hard work for them. Another twenty minutes, and they arrived at the deputy's kist. They looked inside and saw that he was dead.

'He looks as if he's just fell asleep. Look, there's a pencil in his hand. He must have been writ'n his report out,' one said.

Frank slumped to the floor in despair. His breathing came short and fast. Tom knew that Frank was suffering from an anxiety attack, 'Lie doon a minute, Frank, and get thee breath. Try and keep in control. We're not deed yit and ah'll be buggered if we dinna at least try an' get oot of here!'

The two kids in the group, Fred and Bob, seemed to have taken no hurt. Both were footballers and at the peak of condition, so Tom consigned them to look after Frank.

They knew they were only about a hundred yards from the main way, but were reluctant to go because of the smell of burning timber and the fear of more gas being present. They knew that one whiff of firedamp was fatal, yet it was the only chance to get to the shaft and to safety. Tom decided that only two of them should go. One of the young ones volunteered to go with him. They poured water over pieces of material, which they had torn from their shirts, and held them over their mouths.

Tom and Fred cautiously moved off, keeping as low as possible to avoid the choking fumes. Twisted ring girders, which had been blown down, lay in their path. The conveyor belt had broken and hung limp over its rollers. Coal tubs were scattered like dominoes, their contents spread over the way.

The two clambered over the obstacles, being careful to keep low. At last they could see the gearhead. They went past it and on to the 'T' junction. The air was foul, but still breathable. All of the sudden there was a shout. They turned to see dozens of lights coming towards them. There were other miners who had found their way out. They explained that they had been there awhile, deciding to stay where they were and wait for the rescue party, which they were sure would come.

'Have yer tried to gan outbye?' Tom queried.

'Aye, but it's blocked. There's a little opening but smoke's pouring through it. Nor, ah think we'll wait here. Thee bound to knarr what's happened on bank by noo.'

Tom went to look for himself. The man was right. Smoke flowed through the hole. He crawled back to his group, 'The others are wait'n to be rescued, but ah think we should have a try at moving some of the blockage. The ventilation must be still on because it's blow'n the smoke through.'

Frank shook his head, 'It's risky Tom. Ah mean, we not sure what's on the other side.'

Tom put his hand on Frank's shoulder, 'If we get through and beyond whativer's burn'n, there might be a chance that there's clean air. It's only ah dinna like wait'n doon here like rats in a bloody trap. Ah mean, there's a dart's final at the club the neet!'

Normally they would have laughed but they could only manage a forced smile. Blackened, with sweat running down his face, Frank shook his head.

One of the young lads spoke up, 'Haway, Frank, lets 'ave a go. The shaft bottom's not far from there.'

Tom realised that Frank was giving up, 'The lad's reet, Frank. We'll try an' keep as close to the floor as we can and try an' get as far as possible. If it gets bad, we can arlways turn back, but we'll have to mak our minds up soon. Have a couple of minutes to think aboot it. Here, have a drink of watter.'

'It's basic science, man! What's the use of wait'n here? There's nee wind, and there's a good chance of more gas build'n up!' Arthur said who had been silent up till then.

George added, 'Aye, and that means another explosion. Get on thee bloody feet, man!'

Frank's courage reluctantly returned. 'Let's get gann'n then. Tom, what aboot the others?'

'We'll ask them and if thee want to come, there's nowt stopp'n them. Here, use my watter an' soak ya bits of cloth.'

Tom went down and told the men of their plan. They still refused to accept Tom's escape route. No, they would wait for the rescue teams. After a few handshakes the posse of six men set off between the way, which they knew led to the shaft bottom, and they hoped, their deliverance.

Placing the wet pieces of cloth over their faces they ventured through the small hole, clearing the debris as they went. With tears in their eyes they followed Tom. Timber props smouldered. Visibility was only a couple of yards, but they had walked this route for years, back and forth and were at least confident that they knew the shaft was in that direction.

'Keep low lads and breathe through ya wet cloths,' Tom shouted. 'Haway, Albert, gis thee hand.'

Twenty yards, thirty, fifty ... then Albert sank to the ground. Before he could say that they should leave him, Tom ordered the two young lands to hoist him up and onward. Albert did not have the strength to resist. George had gone on to the front and had disappeared into the choking smoke.

'Where the hell's he gone?' Fred asked Tom.

'Never mind, just keep going.'

Three more bodies, badly mangled with twisted expressions on their faces, lay crumpled and partly covered with stones. Tom sensed the two young lads falter as they stared at the pitiful sight.

'That's Harry... and Eric... he has three bairns... and that's the Sparky. They must have been mend'n the panel.'

Tom jerked them away, 'Haway! Nivver mind aboot them. Keep gann'n!'

They all started to be affected by the smoke when they heard a faint shout from George in the distance, 'Haway, it's clearer farther on!'

They struggled towards the sound of his voice, 'Come on!...Come on!'

The smoke started to clear and they approached George who stood by a door.

'Ave had a look and it seems to be clear of smoke, but ah thought ah had better wait till ya caught up.'

Albert was nearly unconscious. The two young lads started to realise the dilemma they were in. 'What if the shaft's blocked?' Fred blurted and Bob joined him, 'The lamps are fad'n. How long will we last without something to eat?'

They opened the door. Fresh air roared around the group. They sat Albert up. He started to recover. 'Dinna fret, lads. They'll be trying to get us oot.'

'All right then, let's away.' Tom wanted to get to the shaft bottom.

There was no further damage. They took their heavy batteries and cap lamps off and sat under the electric lights by the shaft's entrance. Tom took a deep draught of water from his bottle, after giving Albert some. Black and wet with sweat, they gulped in the cold, fresh air and spat the coal dust from their lungs. One of the young lads peered up the shaft then, excited, he ran back to the others.

'The cage is come'n doon, Tom! Come and see!'

Sure enough, there was a pin prick of light coming down the brick-lined shaft. They stepped back as the cage door was wrenched open. The manager of the colliery and a posse of rescue workers stepped out.

They could have made the darts final but they didn't have enough players. The others were still down there.

Glossary

caunch	stone overhang
foreshift	working during the night
gearhead	motor which drives a belt
mothergate	large tunnel
tailgate	small tunnel
way	tub rails
wood chock	support

20TH CENTURY

Even today, Harry Houdini is referred to as the greatest escapologist who ever lived. He made his first appearance in the North East in January 1901. He performed at the New Empire Palace Theatre, in Newgate Street, in Newcastle. The finale to this show was his 'Water Torture Cell', which is still classed as one of the most dangerous feats of escapology.

THE GREATEST SHOWMAN
David Cummings

Robert had polished his boots without being told, and flattened down his thick black curly hair, as he and his father got themselves ready for their evening out.

It wasn't a long walk from their home in Percy Street to the theatre in Newgate Street, but John and Robert were so excited about the evening's show, that it seemed to take them forever to get there. They were going to see Harry Houdini, 'The Greatest Handcuff King and Prison Breaker. No prison or padlock can hold him.' That was what the poster, advertising his arrival from America, said. They were soon in their seats and John read the evening's programme, while Robert studied the newly installed stage lighting, wondering if this invention, called electricity, would ever find its way into their home.

'I can't wait, Father, can you?' asked Robert.

John had noticed movement in the pit at the front of the stage, and realised the orchestra was preparing to play their first tune. 'Look Robert,' he said, pointing at them. 'It won't be long now. The orchestra's almost ready.'

John had only just spoken, when a drum roll resonated around the packed theatre. That led into the overture, which signalled the start of the show, and the appearance of the Great Houdini. Once more the percussionist began a roll on the timpani drums, and then Houdini appeared from the wings. He held out his arms and simply said, 'Welcome everyone. Be prepared to be amazed.'

The drums died down and Houdini walked to the centre of the stage. Robert was so excited, shifting continuously in his seat. He could feel the hypnotic stare of Houdini upon him.

For thirty minutes The Handcuff King amazed the audience as he performed various feats of escapology. The show was gradually building up to the most thrilling finale which Robert, and probably most of the audience, had ever witnessed.

Houdini was a short man with a rounded face, piercing eyes and dark wavy hair, parted down the centre. He surveyed the whole audience, then announced, 'And now, Ladies and Gentlemen. We have come to the part of the show which, I promise you, will remain in your minds forever. However, before we get to that, may I introduce you to my wife and chief assistant, Bess Houdini.'

Bess walked onto the stage and took up her usual position, which was on her husband's right. The audience greeted her with great applause and cheers of delight. Her pearl and diamante covered costume looked more suited for the stage than the every day three piece suit which Harry always wore. He did this intentionally, to give the impression that everything about him was 'normal'. Bess, dressed as she was, provided perfect misdirection at crucial times during the performance! As the applause died away, Houdini clapped his hands twice and a large packing trunk was carried onto the stage.

'I require the assistance of two audience members, to act as witnesses to the fact that this trunk is without any secret preparation whatsoever.'

Instinctively, John leaped from his seat, pushed past Robert and the four people to his right, and ran to the steps at the side of the stage. It took Robert a few seconds to realise what his father was doing, but then he clapped and cheered along with everyone else. John and another gentleman joined Houdini on stage.

Houdini led them both to the packing case and instructed them, in a voice loud enough for the whole theatre to hear, 'Please check the trunk thoroughly.'

John and the other gentleman moved around the wooden crate, hitting the sides, checking joints, and even climbed inside to try and find any hint of a secret panel. Finally John announced to the audience, 'We have checked this trunk, and it is most definitely without preparation.'

'Thank you both,' said Houdini. They left the stage to applause from the appreciative audience.

'I will allow myself to be tied up inside a canvas mailbag, and placed into this trunk,' Houdini announced. 'The lid will then be secured with four steel padlocks, thus preventing my escape.'

With that, Houdini's assistants tied his wrists behind his back with twine, as he stepped into the mailbag. This was lifted over his head and also tied securely. Then Houdini was lifted into the trunk and the lid fastened in place on all four sides with heavy padlocks. Finally a rectangular wooden frame was placed around it, and a four-sided black curtain secured to it, thus preventing anyone from glimpsing the method of Houdini's escape. As soon as the curtain was in place, Bess announced,'We call this next escape: Metamorphosis. Please count to three along with me, and experience the impossible.'

She moved to the front of the curtain, found the slit in the centre and stepped partway inside. With her head and shoulders poking out from the curtain, Bess counted.

'One.' The audience counted along.

'Two.' Still they counted with her. She smiled at them and with a flourish she disappeared inside the curtain.

'Three.' This time the audience didn't count. They were stunned into silence.

The voice counting 'three' belonged to Harry Houdini. The curtain twitched, and he appeared from the same gap which Bess had disappeared into, only moments before. The whole theatre erupted into tremendous applause. Once more Houdini had amazed them with his skill. As he took his bow, the curtain was removed from the trunk, the lid unlocked and the mailbag untied. Out jumped Bess, to an even louder applause, and no one clapped more enthusiastically than Robert. However, there was more to come.

'Ladies and Gentlemen, before I perform my final, and most death-defying, feat for you tonight, there is something I must explain.' From the tension in Houdini's voice the audience could tell that this was serious.

'What you are about to witness, is the most dangerous performance you will ever experience during the whole of your lives. Never before have I demonstrated anything as challenging as my next escape. If, for whatever reason, I should be unsuccessful, and should die as I attempt this, I wish it to be known that I hold neither the theatre management nor my wife, my assistants, or any of you responsible. But if I do succeed, you will leave this magnificent building tonight, knowing that you have witnessed a performance of the greatest and most successful escape artiste, ever. No lock can hold Houdini!'

With that, he turned and walked to the centre of the stage, and the whole theatre cheered and applauded. There was much tension and fear among the audience. Women held their hands to their mouths. Children covered their eyes. The men just sat and pretended that they weren't scared as the Water Torture Cell was wheeled out to meet Houdini. Robert sat at the very edge of his seat, and gripped his father's fingers. He stared straight at the sight before him.

The cabinet was made from glass and filled to the top with water. It was edged in steel, and had a four-inch thick mahogany lid. The glass walls were around seven feet high, three feet wide and two feet six inches deep. Houdini pointed to the tank and announced.

'Within the lid of this glass tank, there are two holes. They are for my feet, which will be shackled and padlocked in place. I will then be hoisted up with the aid of a pulley, and hung upside down, directly over the top of this watery tomb. Then I will be lowered head first into the tank, and the lid will once again be locked into position, thus preventing any possible means of escape. A curtain will be placed around the tank, preventing you from seeing the pain and suffering I will endure while attempting to escape. I will have one minute and thirty seconds in which to free myself from this tomb. Any longer and my lungs will burst, and I will suffer the most horrible drowning anyone could endure. Ladies and Gentlemen, the Water Torture Cell!'

This time, the applause was a lot less enthusiastic. Would he escape, or would he drown? That was the question most of the audience were asking themselves.

Houdini left the stage and reappeared two minutes later, dressed in a bathing costume of blue and white hoops, which looked rather comical on him.

'Please excuse the choice of costume. It appears the theatre management have a sense of humour,' he said, smiling to the audience. This eased the tension a little and some of the audience laughed, though still somewhat nervously.

Robert never moved. He couldn't believe that this man was going to attempt something as dangerous as this, just to entertain him! He crossed his fingers and began to recite a prayer in his head. He hoped that would help Houdini to escape.

Houdini lay on the wooden boards of the stage as his feet were securely locked into the mahogany lid. Chains were then fastened to it, and together they were hoisted into the air and over the opening in the top of the tank. He lowered his arms into the water and wet his face and hair.

'Ladies and gentlemen, please hold your breath with me for ninety seconds. Then imagine struggling to free yourselves from this chamber.'

One of the assistants climbed a stepladder behind the tank and waited to padlock the lid in position.

'I will count to three, I will fill my lungs and diaphragm with oxygen, and when I nod my head I will be lowered into the water.'

The air hung with tension. No one spoke, though a few fidgeted nervously. But not Robert, or his father. They were glued to the sight before them. Robert was worried. He had recited the prayer in his head continuously for the last ten minutes, and intended to continue.

'One,' Houdini breathed deeply. 'Two,' another breath. He looked over at Bess, smiled, winked one eye and shouted, 'Three.'

With that, Houdini took one final breath and nodded his head. The lid was lowered and locked in position. Bess stood at the side of the stage and counted out loud in ten second intervals. The assistants wrapped the chamber with a curtain as Houdini could be seen struggling to free himself.

'Thirty seconds,' Bess announced.

Some of the audience had already stopped holding their breath, others looked nervously at each other. Robert squeezed his father's hand as he noticed the four assistants entering and taking up their position on either side of the tank. They each held a large axe over their shoulders, ready to break the glass, if given the signal from Bess.

'Fifty seconds,' she continued. 'Open the curtain and let us see what is happening.'

One of the assistants laid his axe on the stage and moved to the tank. He opened the front of the curtain, and a disappointed audience could see that Houdini was still securely locked and struggling to escape.

'One minute and ten seconds.' The curtain was pulled over the front of the tank again, and the assistant resumed his position at its side.

'Ninety seconds, ladies and gentlemen. One minute and thirty seconds,' Bess announced slowly. The assistants fidgeted, but she signalled for them to remain in position.

'Two minutes,' she shouted, this time with a worried quiver in her voice.

Robert could stand it no longer. 'Break the glass. Break the glass,' he yelled, as he jumped from his seat, putting his hands to either side of his mouth to amplify his voice.

The theatre manager ran from the back of the stalls onto the stage, and grabbed an axe from one of the assistants.

'For God's sake stop it!' he shouted.

Bess yelled, 'Two minutes and thirty seconds.' Houdini had been underwater, struggling for his life, a whole minute longer than he said he could be.

'Break the glass!' she finally commanded. She stepped to the chamber, grabbed a corner of the curtain and pulled it away from the tank. The whole audience expected to see Houdini suspended in the water and lifeless. But he wasn't. Instead he sat on top of the mahogany lid, with legs crossed, reading a book.

The audience sat stunned into silence. He looked up from his book with a grin and asked, 'What took you so long?'

Once more the whole theatre erupted. Everyone rose from their seats, cheering and clapping this truly remarkable performer.

Assisting Houdini down from the top of the tank, Bess whispered something into his ear. They looked in Robert's direction, and Bess eventually pointed at him. Houdini signalled Robert to join them on the stage. John coaxed the boy from his seat, and Robert climbed gingerly onto the stage. Houdini met him, shook his hand and whispered, 'There was no need to worry, I was never in any danger!'

Robert looked straight into his eyes and continued to shake Houdini's hand. He mumbled, 'You truly are the greatest, Mr Houdini. You are the Handcuff King.'

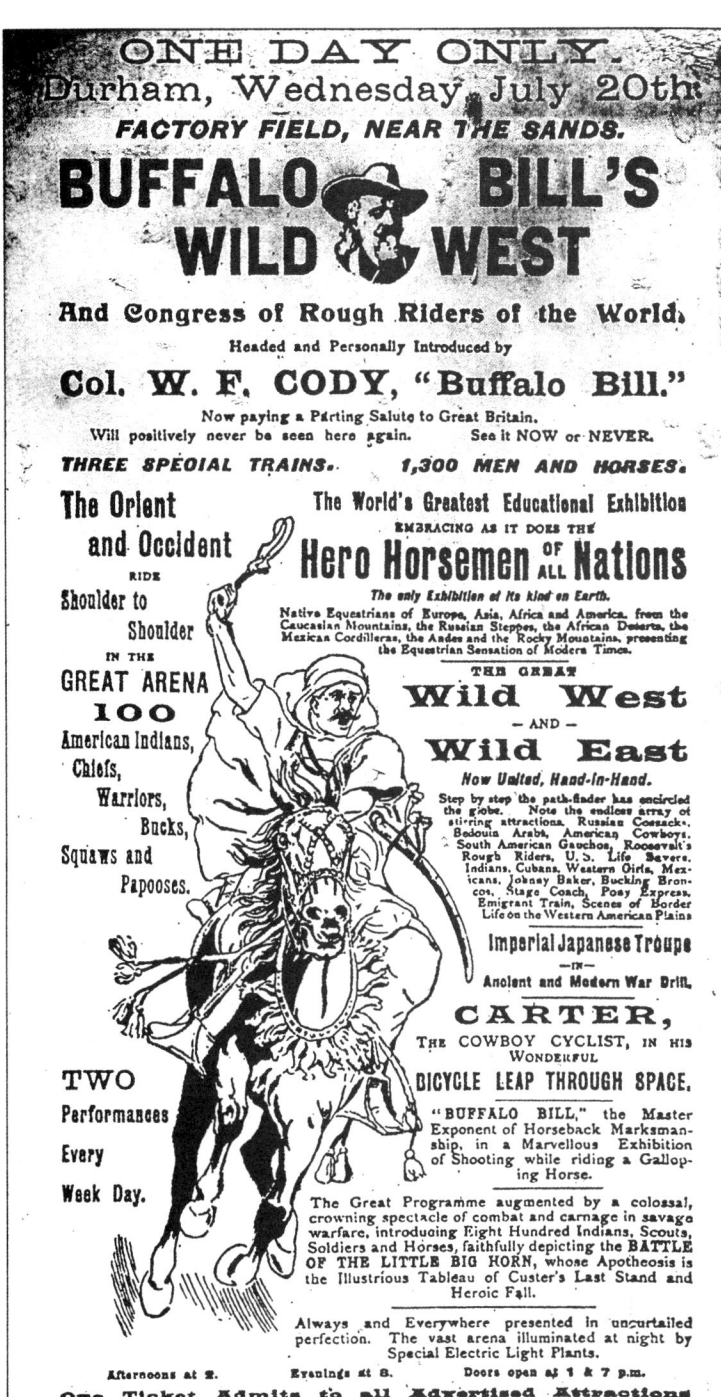

Buffalo Bill had, at least, one personal connection with the North East. Dr. William Adcock, who lived and worked in Quebec, knew William Cody and, maybe, even called him a friend. Trapper, Pony Express rider, prospector, army scout and, finally, showman, Buffalo Bill brought his Wild West Circus to Engine Field, near Elvet Colliery, on 20th July 1904. The circus was a popular form of entertainment at the time. 'If you want to know when the Penny Circus came, take a look at the school attendance records.' There can have been nobody at all in school the day Buffalo Bill's show hit town!

THANKS TO GRANDAD
Sandra Salmon

'God damn the man to Hell and back!'

Adam glanced at Ernie, startled. Their hero had uttered an oath, two in fact. Enough thought Adam, to keep each of them without supper for a week. This, alone, had been worth the two hour walk from home.

He'd have to be careful to be out of earshot of Gran when he told the story to his friends. It was a good job he'd persuaded Ernie to come with him. They'd have to believe the both of them.

Adam parted the canvas, widening the gap, for a better look. Buffalo Bill was striding back and forth, obviously in a fine old rage, and Adam could only hear bits of what he was saying but gathered that a groom had not shown up for work.

The man cowering before Cody's anger said something that Adam could not catch, though he heard the reply right enough.

'Dammit, man. How do I know where ya git anybody at this short notice? That's your job. Go get it done!'

If anyone asked Adam later why he'd done it, he would say that Ernie pushed him. One minute he was spying through a gap in some screening and, the next he was stumbling towards the two men muttering, 'I can groom horses, Sir,' half hoping they wouldn't notice.

However, an Army Scout needs good hearing and Buffalo Bill's was still acute. He spun to face Adam.

'What's that, son?'

Although he was not wearing his fringed buckskin, this close

William Cody was still an imposing figure. He was tall, at least 5ft 10 inches, Adam judged, handsome and immaculately dressed in a flannel shirt and high, polished boots. Adam was disappointed to note there were no spurs, nor did Buffalo Bill sport the wide-brimmed white Stetson. Instead, his hair brown with just a speckle of grey, was worn shoulder length and loose. Adam nervously brushed his hand over his own cropped head and wondered if Gran...no, don't even think it.

'You say you know about horses?'

'Oh yes, sir,' Adam replied firmly.

Buffalo Bill looked for a long moment at Adam and then, not speaking, stalked slowly round him. Until this minute it had not occurred to Adam to wonder what impression Buffalo Bill would have of him, but he questioned it now.

He knew Mr Cody would probably think him older than his years though, at twelve, he was almost a man. He was tall for his age and well muscled but, today, a bit unkempt.

'Let's see your hands.'

Adam's heart sank. He and Ernie had dashed away just as soon as their chores were done, so Adam knew his hands weren't fit to be seen. Gran would be ashamed, he thought, as he held them out for inspection.

Buffalo Bill looked at them for a second or two and, again, solemnly into Adam's eyes. Suddenly he grinned. 'You'll do, son,' and he clapped Adam on the shoulder with a force that had him stumbling forward. 'C'mon, I'll intraduce ya to ma horses.' And Buffalo Bill started to move away.

Adam looked down at his calloused hands and wondered what Mr. Cody had seen that Gran missed, realising as he did so, that he should tell her he'd be late back.

'Wait! Sir! May I send my friend with a message to my Gran? She'll like to know where I am.'

'Sure. Sure, son. I like that. Consideration. Yup, that's good. I'll be in that tent over there. Quick as you can, boy.' William Cody strode off.

'Are you fond or summat?' Ernest Inskip was from Selby.

'Well, I have worked with horses.' Buffalo Bill would have been appalled to hear how apologetic Adam sounded.

'Oh aye? An 'elpin your Granda wi' pit ponies every Sheffield flood meks you an expert, does it?' Ernie held up his hands to forestall any reply. I'll tell your Gran. 'appen she'll not be best pleased wi' me for leavin' you 'ere, but I'll tell er anyroad.'

'Thanks, Ern.' Adam nudged his friend's arm. 'Oh and let's have them carrots you shoved in your pocket before we left, eh?'

'They was me dinner,' Ernie moaned as he handed them over. Thus armed with bribes and tit-bits, Adam ran to find Buffalo Bill and his horses.

Amazed and apprehensive, Adam stumbled to a halt at the tent flap. He had never seen a horse so big that wasn't pulling a plough. The monster nuzzling and nudging at Buffalo Bill must have been seventeen hands, if it was an inch. Just as well there was still time to sneak out.

'Oh, thar' y'are, son. Come an' meet Comanche,' and Buffalo Bill patted the creature's neck. Brave man. It was worse close up. The horse was beautiful, no doubt about it. Gran's cream fudge was just such a colour and its mane and tail sparkled as if woven through with silver thread; but it had feet like manhole covers and nostrils the size of Gran's dustbin lid.

These now flared as the horse blew out, drenching Adam in a blast of warm, grassy breath and then nearly sucked him out of his boots as it breathed in his scent. Satisfied that he was beneath contempt, the stallion turned back to his master.

'This here's Arapaho.' Buffalo Bill had moved down the line to the next horse, which twitched its ears and danced delicately on coal black hooves. It was smaller than Comanche. Not much, but enough to make it more horse than monster. A horse, however, the like of which Adam had never seen. It looked like a pencil drawing with knees, nose, mane and tail coloured black. The rest of its head, neck and body, shaded, as an artist might, to draw out the strength and symmetry of the animal. Then that same artist must have got bored because the horse's rump was peppered with black spots. More spots even than Janey Inskip had produced when she got the measles. Adam gawped and Buffalo Bill, watching, laughed. 'Haven't ya seen an Apalooza before?'

Adam shook his head in wonder as he moved to the last of the three and fell instantly and completely in love.

'This little lady is Cheyenne. I've named them all after Indian tribes to honour our Redskin brothers.'

Adam didn't really listen. He was already besotted with the elegant creature in front of him.

The mare stood about fifteen hands and was the colour of clotted cream. The fine, slightly dished face bespoke some Arabian ancestry. Her eyes were dark and gentle and her muzzle, when Adam reached out to touch her was like cream velvet. Adam's nervousness evaporated. He'd battle the two monsters next door, and a million like them for the privilege of tending this glorious princess of horses.

Buffalo Bill was indicating a bucket and asking if there was anything else he needed. Adam quickly rummaged through the equipment provided. The usual pieces were there; body brush, dandy brush, curry comb, hoof pick and mane comb.

'Sir,' Adam was hesitant about suggesting the equipment was incomplete.

Buffalo Bill waited, eyebrows raised.

'Could I have a sponge, or some soft rags, and some lukewarm water?'

'The water you can git from round the camp,' he turned to go muttering 'soft rags,' under his breath as if he doubted Adam's sanity.

'And, Sir?'

Buffalo Bill stopped but did not turn, 'Yeah?'

'Some neatsfoot oil, as well, please.'

Adam placed his bucket of water well away from Cheyenne and looked at the three horses. They were loosely tethered to a rail, which ran about half the length of the tent. Each horse had an area of about twelve feet wide, separated from its neighbour by a simple canvas screen, which came as high as Adam's shoulder.

There were other horses in the camp that were picketed in lines, western style, but these three, here, had the canvas equivalent of loose boxes. They must indeed be special. They were bedded on fresh straw and seemed to have been mucked out recently — a fact for which Adam was heartily thankful. A pile of cloths, big enough to keep Gran in sheets for a year, had been left in the corner of the marquee. He only wanted to wipe their noses, did they think he wanted to wrap the horses up in them?

As he was nearest to Cheyenne, Adam decided to start with her. His routine would be the same with all the horses and he rolled up his sleeves and began. Adam tore a strip off one of the cloths, dampened it and, gently, cleaned the mare's eyes and nostrils. She looked surprised, but not as surprised as when

Adam reached up and carefully but firmly pulled her ears. It was something he had seen Grandfather do. He called it 'stripping out' and said he didn't know how but it seemed to refresh the ponies. Adam considered simply brushing the mare down, after all she looked clean enough, but he could almost hear Grandad 'tut'. Instead he made himself a wisp, a pad of straw, and began to rub the mare down. Grandad again, 'Better than a brush for getting the tows out — and put some elbow grease into it.'

The mare was a pleasure to work with. She seemed to know exactly when to move to make Adams job easier. He whistled softly as he worked and she appeared to enjoy his tuneless rendering of one of Gran's favourite hymns. She had been, superficially, well looked after but, to Adam's eye the finer points of the grooming art had been missed.

'Flick the mane over, lad. See the dandruff?' Not much, but enough to displease Grandad. Adam wisped harder. The mare's feet were clean and she lifted them neatly and promptly for Adam's inspection. Once again, she seemed surprised when Adam bent and started to hand rub her legs. It was supposed to help the circulation, Grandad said, and Adam wasn't sure it was strictly necessary with these horses but it would do them no harm.

Cheyenne obviously enjoyed it and rewarded him with a soft nicker and by nuzzling the back of his neck as he did her lower front legs. He finished her off with a good brush down and spent a bit of time using the brush on her mane and tail. 'Combs is sloppy practice, lad. Thins the hair and does nowt in the way of cleaning — and put some elbow grease into it'.

Finished, Adam stepped back to assess his handiwork. The mare looked wonderful. Her coat and her abundant blonde mane and tail shimmered like waterfalls in the aqueous light in the tent.

Adam reached into his pocket for one of the tit-bits he had press-ganged off Ernie.

The mare took it delicately, whisking it away as a lady might snatch her hand from the too familiar kiss of an importunate suitor. Adam chuckled and, swinging away to tackle Arapaho, he collided with a Monolith!

It took all of Adam's self-control to prevent himself from squeaking. Where had the man come from? He must have sprung fully formed from the very earth. Adam couldn't breathe without making the straw rustle, but this man had appeared without a sound. He was slightly shorter than Adam and like Buffalo Bill, wore a simple woollen shirt, but the doeskin breeches he wore were fringed and the moccasins on his feet were decorated and beaded with an intricate design in turquoise, red and white.

Adam noticed all this because he found it difficult to face the impassive gaze of someone the colour of Gran's dining-room table and who showed about as much emotion.

The Indian held out his hand, palm up, offering Adam a small jar. 'What's this?'

The Indian managed, without moving a muscle, to indicate a total lack of concern. 'Colonel Cody say you want. I bring.'

In spite of the fractured English, Indian or no, Adam could not see this man as anyone's lackey, so he was carefully polite in his acceptance.

Opening the jar, he sniffed the contents but already knew it as the neatsfoot oil he had requested.

The Indian must have been more curious than he appeared because he nodded at the jar and asked, 'Why you want?'

Adam grinned and turned back to Cheyenne.

'Look, see her feet?'

He softened a pad of cloth with the oil and rubbed a little into one of her hooves. Now every line, every shading glowed and her foot shone like nacre.

'Grandad doesn't approve of us using too much but, when we're showing the ponies off, we sometimes dress their feet like this, see? An' I thought, well, these horses would be wantin' to look their best, like. Wha' dya think?' Adam was talking to himself. The Indian had vanished.

Turning to Arapaho, Adam started the routine again. This time when he'd finished stripping the ears, the horse had shaken its head and rolled its eyes so comically that Adam had laughed out loud.

He found too that Arapaho was much harder work than Cheyenne. Arapaho danced and fidgeted under the wisp and, when it came to checking his hooves, the horse found a wonderful new game. The horse would make as if to lift his foot but, just as Adam bent to pick it up, would drop the weight back on to it and lift the other hoof. Adam finally won the battle by feinting for the off-fore and grabbing the near leg as the weight came off.

Arapaho conceded the match and Adam checked and cleaned the other feet without trouble.

The horse did not seem as appreciative of Adam's repertoire of hymns as Cheyenne, so he continued quietly with the routine, brushing the animal's speckled coat with long, smooth strokes.

He bent slightly, to get at Arapaho's belly and, quick as lightning, the horse's head had whipped round and pulled Adam's shirt from his belt.

Adam sighed as he arched his back, stretched, then tucked his shirt back into place.

He bent again to his work and, whisk, out came the shirt.

Once again, Adam straightened, tucked in his shirt and started to bend but then whirled round, shaking the brush under a surprised Arapaho's nose. 'Don't you dare, my lad, or I'll sing the whole of "The Old Rugged Cross" to you.'

Arapaho thought about this for a moment and, when Adam began to brush his shirt remained untouched. Adam chuckled and patted the horse's rump as he crossed to groom the other side. 'Frightened you, did I? Well, I'm not in the Chapel choir, that's for sure.' Arapaho nodded his head in apparent understanding, which had Adam smiling again.

Grooming complete, Adam offered the carrot tit-bit. Arapaho took it end on and rolled it round his lips for all the world as if he were checking a fine cigar, then, satisfied, he appeared to swallow it whole.

Adam was still laughing over Arapaho's antics and so he did not, at first, register the tension in the last of his horses. Like Arapaho, Comanche fidgeted under the wisp but not with the same happy demeanour. Every time Adam touched the horse it would set up a wave of rippling muscles. A mettlesome horse, thought Adam, but he'd dealt with worse. Thinking about it, as he brushed acres of toffee coloured hair, he realised just how easy these animals had been to work with. What some of the pit ponies lacked in stature, they made up for in temper. 'Born cantankerous and grow up worse' was another of Grandad's sayings.

Comanche was, Adam noted, the least well groomed of the three and he was amazed at how much dust came out of the curry comb when he tamped it out. 'A real fur coat and no knickers job', as Gran would say when she thought little ears weren't listening. Adam had almost finished when some distant, or imagined, noise sent Comanche skittering forward, knocking the brush out of Adam's hand and kicking over the bucket, sending its contents flying.

'Blast,' Adam said loudly, as he reached under Comanche's head to retrieve the bucket.

The wall of yellow teeth that slashed past his arm tipped Adam onto his backside in his haste to avoid them.

He crabbed away, not bothering to get to his feet, only stopping when he felt the canvas wall of the marquee at his back. He stared at the horse, amazed. There was no one in sight. In fact, Adam had been surprised at how few people he had seen. Mr Cody had looked in soon after he had finished Cheyenne, nodded his approval, and left with a smile and a nod for Adam. Later an Indian boy had brought a steaming bowl of something that tasted, suspiciously, of rabbit. Adam daren't wonder where they found the ingredients. The picture of Sioux warriors stalking rabbits across County Durham was more than he cared to imagine. He had enjoyed the quiet company of the horses but now he could do with some help.

He looked across at Comanche. The horse was tense but quiet, its ears pricked towards him. 'Right,' thought Adam, 'back to the fray', but, not wanting to risk those teeth again, he looked for some other means of retrieving the brush. He was lucky. Just visible under a pile of hay to his left, Adam could see the end of a stick. When he pulled he found, to his delight, that it was nice and long. Triumphantly Adam hurried to recover his brush.

Comanche tried to rear, his ears flat to his head and the eyeballs showing half moons of white as the rope halter tautened, then held.

Adam was puzzled. The horse had been difficult, yes, but not savage and, with patience, Adam had even felt he was winning Comanche's confidence. What had caused the change? He looked, again, at the fretful animal and realised that Comanche wasn't looking at him. The horse was watching the stick. Adam laid it, deliberately, on the ground. Comanche stopped shuffling. Adam picked up the stick and, immediately, Comanche threw back his head, straining at the tether. The penny dropped. The horse wasn't vicious, it was frightened and someone, sometime, had beaten it with this very stick. Adam stepped back a couple of paces and, making sure the horse saw what he did, broke the stick into four pieces. Then he strode to the tent flap and hurled them away.

Comanche was standing quietly when Adam returned but he wasn't going to risk teeth or hooves by reaching under the horse for the brush.

Adam opted instead to utilise the hay. He grabbed a couple of handfuls, stood on one end while he twisted them and then doubled it so that he had a nice hard pad. It would have been better damp but never mind. Speaking softly and moving slowly, Adam began gently to smooth Comanche's honey coloured coat with long, soothing, strokes hoping to ease the animal's tension. The horse tossed its head, its ears flicking back, and Adam jumped, but it was nothing he'd done.

Silent as a stalking wolf the Indian had appeared from what few shadows were in the tent.

How long had he been watching and why hadn't he helped? The Indian did not speak but padded slowly along the line of horses. Finally he nodded.

Adam was modestly pleased with the unspoken approbation. He had the feeling he'd been judged and not found wanting. He was even more surprised however, when the man spoke. Gone was the guttural, broken English of earlier. The voice was still deep but the language fluent as he said, 'The other groom. He wasn't ill, or drunk. He couldn't work. I broke his arm.'

Adam blinked and sagged against Comanche's shoulder. He was hardly aware that, this time, there was no nervous reaction. As the horse gently nudged his hand, Adam was ready with the last of Ernie's carrots.

Standing head to head with the placidly crunching Comanche, Adam thought of a thousand questions he would like to ask but it didn't matter. The Indian had gone.

The Great War of 1914-1918 was a conflict which brought about great changes for the women of this country. This story tells of one woman's experience of this time.

DOROTHY'S DREAM
Alice Smith

When Dorothy stepped out of the house into the bitter cold air of the December morning, she had no clear idea of where she was headed. Travelling just a short distance, she left the smattering of stone cottages, their grimy chimneys sending skywards soft tendrils of pale grey smoke, before turning onto a dirt track which led past fallow fields. Only a few weeks before she had been one of the industrious workers bringing in the glut of potatoes and cabbages. The path was wide enough to take the one and only bus, seating twelve passengers, running four times a day to the village of Woodfield, but only once on a Sunday, and today was Sunday.

There was no sun to tempt people out of doors. A strong wind had suddenly taken hold of the day and was cutting across the open fields like a knife of cold steel. Wrapping the fur collar of her winter coat more tightly about her throat, holding it there, letting her face fall into the warmth, she struggled on. The heavy coat flapping against winter boots further hampered her progress, and she was regretting her impulsive departure from the cottage. But, after a night when the war, which had dominated her life since the summer of 1914, had invaded her sleep with terrifying and horrible images, she had felt a great desperation to escape.

She had wakened from the worst nightmare she had ever known. Her ears were reverberating with the thumping of her heart, her hair and nightgown wet from perspiration, and as she struggled to consciousness, a locked scream finding freedom finally woke her. Relief in the realisation that she was safe in her own bed was tempered with reluctance to replay the scene, for she was convinced that her dream had been prophetic, and that within days she would hear that Alex, her husband, was dead.

After three and a half years of war, during which millions had been slaughtered, grey-faced men still clung to the muddy walls of their trenches, rifles spitting death at a faceless enemy across the short stretch of no-man's land. Alex had been in it right from the start. Although married only a few weeks, he had volunteered in a moment of patriotic enthusiasm. Surprisingly quickly, he was sent off to a training camp in the South of England. Determined to make the best of things, he accepted the rigours of army life with good grace. When he learned that he was to be sent to the front, he wrote to Dorothy, asking her to join him in London on his weekend leave.

It had been the happiest of times. There had been no one else in the world other than themselves. Their first experience of London, they had revelled in the excitement of it. The autumn air had retained some of summer's warmth, and in the parks, the presence of late roses lifted their hearts and added to their joy. The tragedy of war had not yet set its stamp on the City's grandeur and as they walked hand in hand through the streets, they felt a part of that grandeur; it was as if they were flying. Momentarily, they would remember why they were there together and tighten their hold on each other, letting the shadow of the war disappear, speaking only of their present happiness. Even their silences were golden. Later they would recall their thoughts at those times and gain comfort from them. But then it was over. They took their leave in the hotel room which had served them so well. In the taxi, taking them to the station, there was nothing more to say. She had asked him to go before the train left. That was the last time they had been together, and the years had passed.

Returning to the cottage which she and Alex rented from John Branton, Dorothy braced herself to face an uncertain future. She spent the first few days in trepidation, unable to focus her mind on anything which didn't reflect images of Alex. This created a tremendous low, in which she allowed herself to flounder, wallowing in the luxury of turning a blind eye to her usual meticulousness in caring for her home. Then one morning she emerged from the fog to the realisation that she was sinking into depression, the lack of motivation a worrying sign. Reluctantly, she forced herself to rid the furniture of its gathering dust. As she worked, her mood lightened. Feeling a surge of energy she spent the rest of the day bringing order to the chaos, seriously chewing over her situation until she arrived at the decision to ask John Brunton to give her work on his farm.

Verging on the 300 acres of farmland stood the farmhouse, two ancient oak trees guarding the entrance. John and Adele Branton greeted her warmly, showing little surprise at her visit. They were fond of her, having watched her grow from early childhood. Dorothy told them of her meeting with Alex in London and of his leaving for France.

'How are you coping then?' Adele asked.

'Well enough! But I've come to ask if I can come and work for you.'

'On the farm?' John scratched at the few hairs on his head.

Adele, looking at John, nodded and said, 'I'll go along with that. After all, we've already been asked to take on one or two land-girls,' then to Dorothy, 'You could be one of them, if that's what you want.'

Over the next few days, Dorothy prepared to move to the farm. Living there, she returned to the cottage only when she had time off; that and the outdoor life were especially helpful in allowing her to overcome the emptiness of the days without Alex. She fought hard not to let the sight of the casualty lists diminish her, pushing the anxiety away, grateful for the long hours demanded of her. Since Alex had left she knew no other life.

The nightmare had struck on the first night of a week's leave. In it, she had been in a mud filled trench, her insides juddering from the booming of the great guns aimed into the path along which she was trying to move. She could not move. Fear gripped her. She stared at a sight too terrible for her mind to comprehend. Against the walls of the trench, as far as she could see, were men, indented into the mud, hanging there, all of them with gaping holes where once had been faces. She stood among others, heaped around her feet, rats and maggots feeding on the putrid flesh of once beautiful sons of proud mothers. Regaining movement, she searched frantically for her husband. Where there was no face to identify, she snatched at hands looking for his ring until, to her despair, she found that all wore identical ones. As she stepped over the dead, rats chewed at her ankles. She tried beating them off, the screams refusing to leave her throat. The grotesque sight of the men without faces gave her the will to run and, as she ran, she found she was running free; the rats no longer there. In fact, a welcome silence had fallen over the trench, the dead men had gone. She stopped running and leaned, breathlessly, against a wall.

Heartbroken, she sobbed. Tears cascaded down her cheeks onto the nightdress she was surprised to see she was wearing. She looked around and caught sight of the figure of a soldier coming towards her. Wearily, he led a donkey loaded with heavy sacks. His head was bare. He was wearing army trousers with puttees and his khaki shirt had the sleeves rolled to the elbows. In that instant she recognised Alex and wanted to run to him. Her legs refused her. She watched as he came nearer and saw that he was smiling at her. It seemed as if he had expected her to be waiting. He stopped, when a few feet away, and his eyes held her eyes. Suddenly, he became a vision of the most dazzling white. There he was, clothed in this brilliant light which illuminated only the spot on which he stood. Then he and the donkey were gone and only the light remained.

She woke to the certainty that Alex would never be coming home again.

Her walk brought her to the farm. She had not noticed the darkening skies and was surprised when the first snowflakes began to fall. They fluttered like soft butterflies against her up-tilted face, their gentle touch soothing. She knocked once quietly and then more urgently when no one came. Disappointed that she could not share her fears for Alex, she decided to continue towards the village and take the bus back home.

With head down against the driving snow, which was rapidly becoming uncomfortable underfoot, she covered the short distance, in time to see the bus arrive outside Campbell's Tea Shop. She considered going for a pot of tea and a scone, but afraid that Joe, the bus driver , might make a quick turn round because of the worsening conditions, she boarded the bus without delay and sat, impatiently willing it to move off.

In spite of the weather Joe waited, obviously hoping for more passengers. Desperately needing to regain the familiarity of the cottage, Dorothy was becoming more irritable and tense, and was relieved when Joe finally decided to leave. Battling against the snow filling his vision, he drove carefully, the journey dragging on painfully. To Dorothy it seemed like a lifetime, but when Joe, ignoring his schedule, turned into her street and put her down outside her front door, she almost wept with relief. Urgently she put in the key.

Before she had shed her coat, she put a match to the fire,

hurrying it along to get a kettle of water going. The mood of the morning returned in full blast, and she felt quite incapable of preparing a meal. She sat by the fire and tried to read to help free her mind of the faceless men of her dream. She kept dozing and stirred herself repeatedly so that she would not fall into a deep sleep, afraid that it might return.

Eventually she slept, and when a heavy knock at the door wakened her, she couldn't place where she was, or what had brought her out of her sleep. The knock came again, loud and insistent. Hesitant, she went to the door. Still half asleep, she failed to ask who was on the other side. She opened it just a little, then wider, allowing the light to fall upon her visitor. A man stood there, every part of him, except his face, completely obliterated by a heavy covering of snow. In blazing white, brilliantly illuminated by the light from the house, he stood there. He hadn't died! He was alive, and he had come home.

In 1926, there was a general strike. However, some people did work through it and this caused many family break-ups.

MORE TEA, DAD?
Tina O'Neill

The cold penetrated the house and the flesh of the girl as she sat on the settee. The fire had been dead for some hours. She remembered how she and her father had spent many a morning together, he as teacher and she as his willing pupil, but still she could not light a fire. The girl felt that this was yet another way in which she had let her father down. But after all, Patrick was her husband, she had to stand by him. So, he worked while her father was on strike. That was nearly twenty years ago. Did it really matter? He was paying now with his life, fighting for his country. Surely, her father could not still hold it against them. This thought made her curl up even tighter in search of her own body heat.

Suddenly there came solid, firm footsteps on the stairs. Her father was getting up. She shivered not from the cold, but from apprehension. She had been visiting her parents for the last twelve years. In all that time, little had been said between her father and her. He always said 'hello' when she arrived, and 'goodbye' when she left, but so much more was left unsaid. They had always avoided being alone together, afraid of what words could never express. They were so much alike, they could never give in. Now they would be alone, their scars there for each other to see. Invisible wounds caused by sharp words from once tender lips. The girl felt the room hold its breath as her father entered. She prayed that someone else would wake up and save her.

Her father stood tall and proud. He stooped slightly now, but was as lean and strong as always. Apart from the stoop the only signs of his age were his silver hair and his heavily creased hands, every crease telling stories of years in the cold, damp bowels of the earth.

He looked at the girl and then at the ashes in the grate. His expression never changed. The girl stood up and moved into the kitchen. She filled the kettle, put it on the gas stove and placed tea in the pot. Her father removed the ashes from the grate. As she washed two cups and placed them side-by-side on the tray with the teapot, she heard him crumple up papers and place them in the grate. Next he would put in the sticks, then the coal mixed with a few of yesterday's cinders. He would light it with a match taken from the top shelf, kept there, safe from small hands. Now he would place the blazer up against the grate to draw the fire to life. He had made the blazer himself. A tear rolled down her cheek as she remembered kneeling beside him in the back-yard, while he made the handle. He had smiled at her then and she had felt warm and safe. She wiped her eyes and busied herself making the tea, as he entered the kitchen to wash his hands. He then returned to the fire and swept the hearth. As the girl poured the tea, he sat in his chair and read the paper. She carried the tea in and placed his cup on the floor beside his chair, then she sat back on the settee and watched him.

His paper shook gently in his hands. It took time for him to turn the pages, and he held it just a little closer to his face than he used to. Who would dare tell him he needed spectacles? He folded his paper and carefully placed it on the chair arm. He stood and looked at the girl, then moved towards the fire. The blazer was now glowing red with the heat of it. He took hold of the handle and walked slowly from the room into the kitchen. She knew that he would walk through the kitchen and along the passage to the backdoor. He would open it and place the tin by the back steps, then he would close it and return to his chair and his paper. The girl had witnessed this ritual many times. As her father returned to his seat he picked up his cup and drank the contents, watching his daughter over the rim of the cup as he did so. He then placed the cup on the floor and reached for his paper.

'More tea, Dad?' she asked.

He grunted in reply. As she walked towards him, he picked up his cup and handed it to her. He did not look up from his paper. As she walked from the room, he turned the page once more.

Marshall Riley's Army is about David Riley, who led the Jarrow Crusade in 1936. In this story David Riley has been asked to talk to a group of students in the lecture theatre of a local University in the early 1980s, and this is what he may have told them.

MARSHALL RILEY'S ARMY
David Cummings

'It was the 5th of October 1936, and we had nothing, and I mean nothing. Steelworks, shipyards, everything was finished. Even the local Conservatives supported us marching to London. I remember a fella called Whittaker. He was a Major or something, and he was the Conservative agent for Sheffield. He even made a statement to the newspapers; I've got it here somewhere.'

The old man fumbled with the papers in front of him, and eventually held up one of them close to his face. The paper looked worn and grubby from the many times it had been held in those once strong hands. He cleared his throat and read out loud, in his best 'upper class' voice.

' "I say this march is a good thing. No matter whether my party's head office likes it or not. These people are bringing to the notice not only of Britain, but of the whole world, that they are fighting for the right to work and the means to live. There can be no politics when people are fighting for their bread and butter."

'You see, we had no money, and that meant the local businesses had very little trade, so a person's politics meant nothing. Some of the lads said it would be the first time they'd been out of Jarrow! We hit a lot of resistance though. Not from the local politicians mind you, but from that lot down in London. They tried everything to stop us once they got wind of what we were planning.

'They said we were wasting our time, that they wouldn't meet us when we got to London. We had this petition for them, you see. We wanted to hand it over to them personally. The lads carried it all the way down in a wooden chest. More than eleven thousand people signed it, and we were going to make sure the politicians got it.

'I remember talking to Guy Waller and Bill Sternberg; two local journalists who followed the march from start to finish. Bill said to me that he'd always felt the shipyard was the life blood of Jarrow. It didn't matter if a man was a labourer, or a top executive. When that yard closed down they were all out of work.

'You see, there wasn't much chance of them finding work anywhere else, because the rest of Northumberland and Durham were depressed as well. Guy said that Palmer's shipyard had been the mainstay of the town. The Company brought a man called McGowan in from Scotland. The shipyard, which had been struggling for some time, was very quickly run down, and there was a saying in Jarrow.

"St. Bede founded it, Sir Charles Palmer built it, and McGowan buggered it."

Riley chuckled, and the whole class joined in. He enjoyed these talks. They allowed him to reminisce to a new audience each time. Not like his old mates down at the Club.

'We got called communists, agitators, and anarchists. All we wanted was work, and to take a bit of money home to feed the family. Some families were surviving on coppers, sent home by their kids who had gone into service down in London, and on handouts from the Public Assistance Committee. At one of the meetings we had arranged to organise the march I said that when Mussolini shouted hard enough, he got our government to lift sanctions against Italy. So if Mussolini could do that, then it was time we showed them that we wouldn't sit there, and swallow the lies they wanted to feed us. They didn't want to know about people living here in Tyneside, under conditions that no respectable farmer would keep his pigs.

'I remember Paddy Scullion saying that he got into trouble of the Labour Party, because he said, the unemployed didn't have the intelligence of a dog. What he meant was that if a man is hungry, he stands looking at food in the shop window. But if a dog is in the same position, he goes in and steals it!

'Aye, they were hard times all right. All we did have was pride, and I could see that it was beginning to weaken by the time they put me in charge of the operation. They made me the Marshall. Marshall Riley they called me.

'They were going to call it the Jarrow March, but I said it wasn't a good name for it. Other marches had been held which hadn't been very well received. So, I suggested we call it a crusade: The Jarrow Crusade.

'On the morning of the march, everyone gathered. It seemed like all of Jarrow, and more, had come to see us. We'd be away more than a month, so families and friends came to see us off. Paddy was there, talking to Mayor Thompson and Ellen Wilkinson, our M.P. Red Ellen she used to get called. We said it was because they thought she was a Communist, but it was really because of her ginger hair. She marched with us all the way. Some of the Councillors, and the Labour and Conservative party agents for Jarrow, travelled ahead of us. That was to make sure all arrangements for food and sleeping were in order. There were two hundred of us and we all needed grub and sleep. Mind you, we originally talked of taking thousands of men with us, but we soon realised that would be too many to feed and look after.

'I was walking around talking with Sam Rowan, when we bumped into Ritchie Calder, the reporter. He asked us, if we had time to talk with a family he'd been interviewing. He took us over to meet them, and I still remember what the father said to us: that the four of them would have liked to march to London with us, but only one of them could.

'So, what they did was this. William and Arthur, his two sons, had given the jacket and the trousers, his brother the raincoat, and he had given the boots. He said that only William was going, but by doing this, it felt as if the whole family marched as one man. That was the fighting spirit of Jarrow.

'So, off we went. We carried that petition in the box, and never let it out of our sight until the end of each day, when the local police locked it in the station, until the following morning. We had two banners with "Jarrow Crusade" painted on them, and a band of about a dozen harmonica players marched at the front every day. It felt as if we were going off to war, which I suppose we were in a way. I'll tell you something else as well. We were so well fed on the way down, that some of us were fatter when we got to London, than we had been when we set off. Everywhere looked after us, they made sure we had a good feed, ready for the next day's march.

'I remember stopping at one town, and Sandy Powell was working at the local theatre. Sam Rowan had been asked to go along and meet him. Anyhow, Sam had been away for about an hour, and when he came back, he had the biggest grin on his face that I have ever seen. He came straight over to me, and I soon found out why. You see, when Sandy Powell asked to meet him, it was to tell Sam that he had reserved two hundred tickets for that night's show. Anyhow, the theatre manager couldn't let him have the seats, as there were too many people already queuing outside. But Sandy told him not to worry, because as soon as the show was over, the whole cast were coming over to the field where we were camped to entertain us there.

'I couldn't believe it, but it was true. They all rolled up in taxis and performed their full show, right in that field. What a night we had!'

Old Riley looked up at the students, their pencils busy scribbling notes and he smiled.

'Anyhow, we eventually arrived in London, and we were all expecting to prove something. Expecting to prove to the capital that we weren't going to let that lot walk all over us. We were going to put our case wherever we could. We organised a big rally in Hyde Park. People from all over London came to hear us. Hundreds of them turned up. But even better, was that all of our kids who were working in London, were given some time off to come and see their fathers, uncles, brothers and cousins. There were a lot of tears shed that day. They wouldn't be going back home to Jarrow. They had to stay and earn a bit of money while they could.

'The government did all they could to avoid us. Mind you, it didn't take long for them to realise we weren't going to go away. I think Red Ellen helped a bit with that as well. They still tried to foil us, though. They gave us a visit around the Houses of Parliament and then most of the lads, and the journalists, went off on a boat trip. That's when they got me to give them the petition. I told them though, we'd be back, and back we were.

'The very next day we threatened to hold a sit-down-strike, right there at the Houses of Parliament. Before long we sat in committee room fourteen, excited and hopeful, and probably a bit scared as well. There were about two hundred M.P's from different parties and just a few of us. Our Mayor, Billy Thompson, had been explaining about the conditions in Jarrow, and how the people were just demoralised, and I thought he had done a good job. But then, he made a speech which made the hairs on the back of my neck stand up, and on a few others, I bet. In fact, I've got a copy of it here, I'll read it out for you. Now you have got to imagine this plump, grey-headed man, standing in his 'best' suit - carried all the way down for this occasion - gripping the mayoral chain of office on either side of his neck, and saying this: "My chain of office was given to Jarrow by Sir Charles, Mark Palmer, who owned our shipyard. Its links form a cable, and its badge is an anchor. Symbols in gold of the cables and anchors, of the thousand ships we built in Jarrow. But now, owing to the National Shipbuilders Securities Limited, the Jarrow shipyard is closed. No longer will ships for this country's food and our defence be made in that yard. God grant that the time will not come when you, Members of Parliament, will have to regret that. You, yes, you allowed the scrapping of this great national asset! In the interests of the profits of a bank's already rich shareholders! Thirty five thousand people starved for pounds, shillings and pence. If you are not going to help these people, then this chain means nothing!"

'That committee room was silent, and then we were brought back by the thud and a clatter of what sounded like a riveter's hammer. Mayor Thompson had lifted the chain from his neck and dropped it onto the desk in front of him, and he stood glaring at every one of those M.P's. Aye, they all knew about Jarrow that day.'

Riley sat back in his chair and looked into the group of students. One of them, a young girl of about nineteen, held up her hand and gingerly asked him, 'Did this crusade do you any good, Mr Riley?'

He shifted in his chair and smiled at her, 'I bet that's the question you all wanted to ask. Is it?'

Almost the whole group nodded as one, and a ripple of laughter went around the room.

'Well, it was like this,' he said, 'We certainly felt better for going down there, though there was no immediate improvement in employment. It took Hitler and the War to do that. We weren't good enough to work but, by God, they soon called us up to fight. Mind you, there was something else which was going on, that we never ever realised.'

Riley grinned the sly grin of an old fox, and continued.

'You see, Ramsay Macdonald's constituency was Seaham Harbour, which was owned by the Londonderrys. Lord Londonderry was a friend of no other than Adolph Hitler, and for thirty days - and quite by accident - The Jarrow Crusade had become a threat to what we have since called "The Fascist Connection." But that, well, that's another story.'

One of the many hair-raising stories from my Uncle Albert, just before he died.

UNCLE ALBERT AND THE D.L.I.
Ron Gray

Albert's eyes flickered open. He felt as though he had been hit on the back of the neck with a sock full of ballbearings. He licked his parchment-dry lips before his eyes rested on the face of a pretty girl who stood at the foot of his bed, smiling. He braced himself against that God-awful pain in his lower stomach.

'What did you give me?' Albert managed to croak.

The pretty girl picked up a chart, 'It's got a hell of a long name, Albert.'

'It doesn't really matter, pet. But ah'll tell tho summit: It's almost worth have'n the pain to experience the feeling of relief ah have now.'

A voice from beside the bed made him turn his head, 'That's a novel way of putting it, Mr. Burns. I've never heard that one before.'

Albert found himself looking at a dark skinned young man in a white coat who took hold of Albert's wrist and stared at his watch for a few moments, 'How old are you, Albert?'

Albert looked down at the doctor's ragged trainers, 'The question is: How old are you?'

'Don't worry, I have all the necessary papers ... How long have you had that bullet in your back?'

'1944.'

'Does it bother you?'

'You needn't humour me, ya knarr. Ah'm not senile or stupid, and ah'm not frightened of death.'

The doctor smiled, 'Only part of the spiel, Mr. Burns. Do you want anything?'

'Aye, ah would like that nice lass to get me a cup of tea .... Oh, aye and I'm 83. And something else, Doctor.'

'You want to run off with her?'

'Besides that.'

'Fire away.'

'How long?'

'How long?'

'So ah can be ready.'

The doctor removed his glasses from his top pocket and started to clean them, staring at the polished squares of linoleum. He looked up and shrugged his shoulders.

Albert broke the silence, 'Ah 'ave to know, because there's the insurance to sort out and everything. My wife'll not be able to cope, so ah'd rather be prepared.'

The doctor stood, 'A month, maybe less.'

Albert seemed to breathe a sigh of relief. The doctor also looked relieved and sat back down, 'We'll see that you don't suffer, Mr Burns ... Look, I have an hour before I go on duty, so why don't you tell me how you got that bullet in the bottom of your spine.'

The nurse came back with the tea and Albert sipped a mouthful, then lay back on his pillow and remembered ...

One day we were at the pit and the next day we were in the D.L.I. Quick as that. God, 1944. Ah could jump a five-bar gate without taking a run. There were four of us, just teenagers. Frightened to death we were. Never saw a dead body before we got to France. When it became commonplace we realised that we could almost laugh about it. How obscene is that? And ya know what? Some of the poor buggers never fired a shot. Their rifles were cocked but they were cut down before they could fire a round off. They would walk up the middle of a street in broad daylight ... All that way ... Some of them hadn't started to shave ... We trained together under this sergeant, who was definitely mentally disturbed...

Macca heard the rumble even before it turned the corner. He took his helmet off and pressed his stubbly beard close to the shattered window. The tank came into view. Macca felt his stomach churn. The tank climbed onto a pile of rubble at the bottom of the street and sat there like a fat toad. It's engine gave a roar, blue exhaust belched out from its back-end before the engine died. Macca looked around the bedroom. Albert sat on the floor with his back to the wall, cleaning his harmonica. Harry had the only undamaged chair, studying photographs in a three week old newspaper. The only French he knew had been picked up in a brothel, along with a dose. Little Bobby lay, face down, on the bed. His right arm hung limp, nearly touching the floorboards. He was snoring loudly.

Macca spoiled their relative peace, 'Harry, wake that bastard up, will yea?'

While Harry shook Bobby, Albert crawled to the window, 'What's the matter?'

Macca showed him the tank.

'He looks as though he's takk'n his bear'ns.' Albert whispered.

Harry and Bobby joined them.

Macca lit a cigarette, 'Better wait and see. He might just be watch'n for any movement.'

Sure enough, a German officer gingerly opened the turret and scanned the ruins with binoculars. He eased himself out and clambered over the tank, jumping on to the rubble. Walking around the rear of the tank, he bent and examined it.

A shot rang out, whining past Macca's ear. It pinged off the tank's side, just missing the officer.

'The stupid sod!...Now he knows we're here!' Macca shouted.

The officer leapt on the tank and quickly disappeared inside. Almost immediately the tank roared into life; followed by a whirring sound as the 88mm gun moved around on its turret. It was aimed at the unseen sniper.

Little Bobby, his tired eyes now wide open because of the huge surge of adrenaline, started collecting his gear, 'Haway lads, before he sends a round up!'

The words hardly left his mouth, when the tank bucked violently on its tracks. The house just above them exploded. The shell created its own shrapnel, made up of bits of brick, plaster and slivers of wood which scythed through living flesh and bone.

As the dust cleared, it found the four trying to make themselves a part of the floor. Almost as one they thundered down the stairs. They made their way to the back door. Albert was last and, out of the corner of his eye, he noticed one of his regiment cowering under the stairs. His hands covered his ears, his knees nearly touching his gaunt face.

Albert tried to pull him up, 'Tho canna stop here, man! Get on thee feet!' He tried to make him stand but the soldier only curled himself up into a ball. Macca looked back and said, 'Leave him Albert. We haven't time.'

Albert stared into the soldier's face and thought he looked like a wounded animal.

Broken slates covered the once tidy garden. The machine gun from the tank rattled, spitting, breaking shards of brick and glass as it raked the sides of the battered houses. The smell of cordite and burning timber made the group venture out into the walled garden.

Bobby shook his head, 'Where did they get the bloody tank?'

Macca's groan was audible even above the din, 'Walter Wilson's, Marks and Spencers! Who cares, ya daft sod.'

Harry laughed, then stopped himself, 'We can't stop here. We have to move further up the street.'

Macca held his hand up for attention, 'Ah'l try and get over, say, four walls. Right? Somebody cover me.'

The other three nodded. Macca very slowly raised his head.

'Right, see the garden with the glasshouse in? Follow me there, one by one.'

Another explosion. More choking dust rolled down the staircase, enveloping them. Albert tapped Macca on the shoulder. 'Go on, young'n, we'll meet up there.'

There eyes met for a brief moment. The bond and total trust in that space would have easily burned through armoured steel plate.

Macca ran and scaled the wall and then another till he reached the garden with the glasshouse. The other three followed.

Macca looked and stared down the street, 'Ah don't believe it. The buggers are brewing up!'

Albert crawled beside him, 'They must think they've cleaned us out. We'll wait till morn'n and make our way back the main road .. 'Ere, what's that blood off Macca?'

Macca looked down at his tunic and saw that a circle of blood was growing larger as they spoke.

'Ah thought ah felt a bump or summit.'

Albert made Macca get away from the window and lie on a coat. He tore away at Macca's tunic and shirt. The wound was just below his heart. Albert stuffed field dressings over it. Still the blood pumped down Macca's front.

Outside, the darkness tried to cover up the ruins, but moonlight cast jagged shadows over the heaps of rubble.

The blood had subsided a little, but Macca was now ashen. The others came over to where he lay and stared.

Bobby shook his head, 'Ya wouldn't have thought that a little piece of lead would 'ave brought down a big man like Macca.'

Harry agreed, then reminded them, 'Can ya remember when he saved us all from that bloody lunatic in Dover? He could 'ave left us there. It wasn't even his fight... When we move out me and Bobby'll carry 'im between us.'

Albert told them to get some rest. He would see to Macca and the window. He sat with his back to the wall.

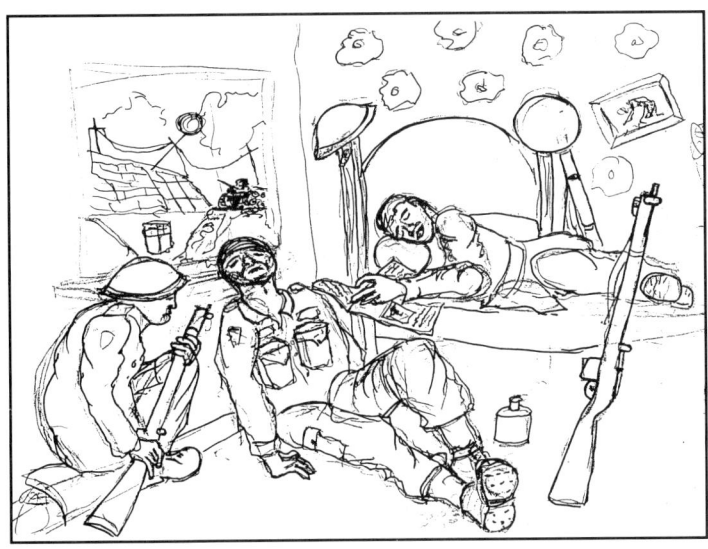

Macca opened his eyes, 'How's that bit stuff of yours, Albert?'

Albert turned, 'Ah thought ya were asleep ... Probably out with one of them Italian POWS. Ya knarr what she said to me on the station? If ya can't be good, be careful. Good, be careful? Around here? That's a bloody laugh. We'll be lucky to see our bloody unit again!'

Macca reached down and pulled a folded card from his trouser pocket. He handed it to Albert, 'Write to my daughter, Albert.'

'It's a Xmas Card ... It's June, ya daft sod. How long 'ave ya been carry'n this about?'

Macca, his voice almost a whisper, 'Write on the back, Albert. Ya know what to write. Ah'm bloody hopeless. Me daughter's name is Moira. Tell 'er ah love 'er and all that... yer know... tell her everything's OK ...'

'What about ya wife, Macca?'

'She left two years ago with an accordion player from the Metropol. Ah knew when ah married 'er. Isn't lads daft when it comes to a bit skirt, Albert? They only have to show us a bit leg and we go loopy. We nearly fought to the death over 'er. He was a waste of good grub, but she chose him anyway.'

Albert laughed, 'It's called poetic justice, young'n. Wait'll he starts practising the bloody accordion till two o'clock in the morn'n.'

Macca wrapped his huge fingers around Albert's forearm, 'Tell 'er to stick in at school, Albert.'

Albert wet the pencil on his tongue, 'Who's write'n this? You or me? Had thee wisht, man!'

Albert sat back and looked up at the ceiling for a good minute then started to write on the back of the Xmas card. Faint music could be heard coming from the tank through the still night air.

Albert quietly read the letter to Macca:

'Sorry for not writing before but I'll make it up to you when I get back. Try not to worry about me and stick to your school work. After this is over they are going to need special people like you. I thank God every day for giving me such a wonderful human being. When I come back I promise that I will never be out of your sight. And if the worst should happen, always remember and hold your head high.

P.S. Please find two pounds enclosed. Your loving Dad.'

'Well, is your Lordship satisfied?' asked Albert.

Macca smiled, 'Two pounds? Where have ah got two pounds?'

Albert leaned forward, 'Don't tell the others, but when we first joined up ah used to cheat at Brag. Ah must owe ya thousands. Ah can spare a couple of quid out o' that.'

'You've got a way with words, Albert, ya big liar.'

Albert lit a cigarette and put it in Macca's mouth. 'If ah can kid our lass, ah can kid any bugger ... Get some rest while ah see what those two buggers are up to.'

* * *

Albert took a sip of orange juice. The doctor could hardly wait, 'And did you get out?'

'Aye, we waited till about three o'clock and sneaked up the back street, when Macca died. Ah hope they took good care of him. Such a waste.'

The doctor shook his head, 'Do you realise Albert, that you've seen more life in ten minutes than a hundred men in a lifetime?... But what about the bullet?'

Albert took another sip, 'When we got to the road, Little Bobby was so chuffed, he tripped over a bit of barbed wire and shot me up the arse.'

'Eyes bright, wattles white, legs of a bright red colour'
Above is the beginning of a rhyme used by my father-in-law, which outlined the qualities by which he judged homing pigeons.

A TEAM OF EXPERTS
Betty Bone

It was Sunday; the one day of the week that miners could devote almost entirely to their favourite hobby and for many, that was keeping and flying pigeons. Sammy Briggs, Marty Hibbard and, fresh from his church at the end of the village, Barney McKenna were men with a mission. It was for sight of Bill's most recent fledglings that they came crunching up his garden path.

Marty, who stepped uninvited into the pigeon loft, called out over his shoulder to the others, 'Ah say lads, howay hev a look at this squeaker.'

William, who had been allowed for the first time to handle his pigeon which had been a tenth birthday present, guarded her with his small hands. He was afraid that Marty might touch her and damage her feathers. There was no need for such concern. Marty was no great scholar but his knowledge of handling and caring for his birds was extensive. Nonetheless, William decided to set Three Stripes on a perch out of harm's way.

Seeing how protective of the bird the boy was, Marty guessed that it would be his, and he began to tease, 'Is this the one yer Da's ganna sell me, then?'

'Behave Marty.' This from Barney McKenna, who had popped his head into the loft. 'Aye, Bill always hes sum lovely lookun' bords, hes'n 'ee. Nee wonder he mak's a good judge. Mind that'n luks a real beauty.' Barney cast an experienced eye over the young bird.

Judging from the exaggerated jerking of her head and the extra brilliance in her eyes Three Stripes, it seemed, was determined to impress the visitors even further. The bird was obviously enjoying the attention and was being a real show-off.

One of the trio was yet to make his comments. Sammy Briggs was still outside, talking to Bill. Sammy was treasurer of the Homing Society and Bill was secretary. Both of these men had been born two generations too early to benefit from an education system by which they could have reached their full potential. Each had also served in the First World War. Bill had been in the Hussars. Sammy's war had been spent in the trenches. Following this experience with working in the mines was beginning to affect his health. Neither spoke of their wartime experiences. These were best forgotten. Even so, both remembered them vividly and each hoped that the current crisis would not last long enough to drag their own children away into the conflict.

'Is she yours, this one?' Sammy having got the information from Bill, indicated the bird that William had been holding. It was an elegant bird with three white bars on each wing. William nodded, unable to conceal his pride in the choice of name, 'She's called Three Stripes.'

Sammy's face registered approval although privately he felt, that if it had been his choice 'Sergeant' might well have sprung to mind, due to the fact that they lived so near to the castle, which was the Headquarters of the Durham Light Infantry. Especially, as soldiers from the nearby camp were passing daily.

But it was Three Stripes who took up residence in the same loft as Melon Hen, now the matriarch. Last year, prior to the beginning of the war, Melon Hen had won what was known as the water race from France.

Another of Bill's birds, Nevers, was similarly distinguished. To be successful in one of these water races was a great achievement, as these were very long-distance contests. William had seen proof of their success, in the gold medals that were at home. Each was kept in its own velvet box. Due to Bill's success, members of the Langley Moor Homing Society were interested when new birds were hatched at his loft. Competition was fierce among those miners who chose to adopt the sport as a hobby.

After Sammy had also looked at the birds, the men assembled outside the loft, crouching on their unkers (haunches). This posture was familiar to men of the mining community. It was the manner in which they sat when waiting to go 'in by' to their work. While they talked William stayed inside the loft, content to be with the pigeons. Presently he was aware that another visitor had arrived and he heard Sammy's 'Morning Major', as he greeted the most recent members of the Langley Moor Homing Society. The one greeting was directed at two men, each one a major; each returned his greeting. Major Banks of the D.L.I. had arrived with his opposite number, Major Berry of the Duke of Wellington's Regiment. Both were currently stationed at Brancepeth. By now all of the men were on their feet.

Marty spoke again. He could always be relied on, to keep conversation on the boil, when a lull would occasionally have been preferable. 'Ah hear you've been gett'n yersel's a few canny bords.'

Major Berry might well have just heard the language of some remote tribe, but smiled and nodded, hoping it was appropriate. When Major Banks answered, his fellow officer was able to deduce that his own gesture had not been amiss.

The officers wanted to fly pigeons with the Homing Society and in consequence, needed to be members. Once accepted, as with any other member, a record of the precise position of their loft was required for the Society documents. Arranging and documenting the information was the responsibility of the secretary, namely Bill. And so it was, that the two officers visited Bill that day. Telephones, of course, were not the norm for the masses at the time.

William hadn't known the purpose of the visit, but he did hear Major Banks refer to him. 'Bring the boy with you, Bill. It'll be an experience.'

As soon as the majors were out of earshot, William wanted to know what had been planned for him but apparently the outing was to remain a secret, for the time being at least. Even his mother wouldn't say where he was going. He did find out that he was going out with his father, on the day his mother went to help at the British Restaurant. The restaurant had at one time been a shop in High Street, where William lived. It had opened after the beginning of the war and the odd meal that could be taken there helped to supplement the rations, particularly useful when food and the week's food coupons were running low.

The day dawned and William's mother and father went off in different directions: William with his father, who was carrying a very large cardboard tube. William knew what was in the tube. He had seen it spread out over the kitchen table several times. The map, which was very large, pinpointed the lofts of all the members of their Homing Society. He was beginning to work out the day's plans.

They didn't wait for a bus. Buses were now so infrequent that Bill and his son would probably reach their destination long before one arrived. Besides, if the bus seats were occupied, William would have had difficulty in standing. At the time one row of seats was lined up and down each side of the vehicle, to leave a large central area for standing passengers. This way more passengers could be accommodated and fewer buses required. Many of the drivers had gone to war and lady bus drivers were as yet an unknown breed. The unfortunate passengers whose lot it was to stand were obliged to hang on to leather straps suspended from the ceiling of the bus. A sharp turn sometimes resulted in a standing passenger losing his or her grip and being catapulted onto the lap of one of the seated. An unpleasant experience, or perhaps even pleasant, dependent on the landing spot or point of view.

In just over two miles along the road, they walked into the lane which led down to the castle. The map had been a real give-away as to the purpose of the day's outing and now of course, William was certain of the destination.

'The castle's down here isn't it Dad? Are we going in? Where are the pigeon crees?' William didn't wait for an answer but continued to chatter as they passed a row of small picturesque cottages. He didn't notice them. 'Do you think Three Stripes will be wondering where we are, Dad?'

'She'll probably be asleep while we're gone,' Bill said, thinking that the poor bird would be glad of some rest from his constant chatter and admiration.

William's eyes were fixed on what was ahead. Bill told him that they were going to mark the position of the Majors' loft on the big map he had brought. William nodded knowingly. He didn't say that he had figured that out some time before, not wanting to spoil the surprise. Soon they reached the castle and still no sign of pigeon lofts.

William had never been so close to the castle before, even though it was so near his home. Today, he stood looking up at the two round towers which flanked the arched entrance to this formidable and uninviting building, his slight figure dwarfed by their bulk and height. Bill pointed out the tower that housed the pigeons and William was left to wonder at the birds being deprived of a proper cree. The tower certainly was a surprise.

From where he was standing with Bill he could hear the gentle murmurings of the pigeons. It surely was the loftiest loft in the area.

As Marty, Barney and Sammy as members of the Committee had arrived, Bill walked towards the arched entrance and handed something to the soldier on duty there. A small room was tucked into the side of the arch and it was from there that a sergeant came out to speak to him. Bill had been introduced to the sergeant on a previous occasion and recognised him as the one who looked after the pigeons at the Castle.

Presently, William and the four men were conducted through the entrance into the forecourt of the castle and after a brief meeting with both Major Banks and Major Berry, they got down to the task in hand.

William was intrigued that one of the officers had instructed the sergeant to take them to the Sergeant's Mess for a meal when they had completed their task. The men accepted and thanked the officers.

'That's arlreet, mind. Yer ganna hev yer dinner in a Mess,' Marty said to William.

Not understanding the word 'Mess' in army terms, William wasn't sure if he wanted to eat there. He wondered for a brief moment whether he would rather wait and have something to eat at home, or even at the British Restaurant. But the thought was quickly forgotten. He was keen to see the pigeons but of course, they wouldn't be as beautiful as Three Stripes. Soon, the sergeant took them up into the tower by a spiral staircase, another first for William.

'Mind arl tell yer what; the bords us ganna hev a heed start from here,' Marty joked with the sergeant.

Having established that the pigeons were there, it was time to do the important work of the day. Bill was soon about the business of pin-pointing the loft, on the large map, which the other men had spread out on an area of grass in the forecourt. There were measurements to be taken and notations to be made. Even Marty was very serious about his responsibilities.

Indication of the lofts on the map took until almost lunch time. The map was carefully rolled and Bill was reinserting it into the tube when the sergeant returned to escort them to The Mess for lunch. William went along obediently but still doubted whether he could eat there. He wondered why his father had agreed so readily. Neither Marty nor Barney had experienced army life and it came as something of a shock to see food set out in such large quantities

'Yae wadd think thee were ganna feed the five thoosand,' Marty was amazed.

'Why nivvo mind just yae eat eenyuff for one man, that'll dee'.

Barney, equally unused to the procedure, followed the sergeant.

It was, after all, a good lunch but William still hadn't worked out why the area where they ate was called the Mess. His remark that it wasn't really messy at all, brought a smile to the others. He was beginning to feel tired after the walking, then eating. Not too tired to notice the two soldiers who were just coming through the door. They still wore hats. Quite different, he thought, from any soldier's hats he had seen before. He knew that Major Banks wore a hat which, was much the same shape but it didn't have a red top like these. The day was full of surprises. A big surprise was yet to come.

The newcomers headed in their direction. After speaking to the sergeant in a manner that William thought was very bossy, one of them picked up the tube containing the precious map.

Marty, true to character, was quick to react and obviously unaware of the authority of the red caps. He was quickly on his feet.

'How, lad, wat'cher dee'un. That's private property. Pur it back.'

The other men were, for the moment, silent. Two of them at least knew that it wasn't quite the way you spoke to Military Police: not, if you didn't want to antagonise them. Marty soon got the message. When one of them turned and glowered at him, he shrank by almost a foot and promptly sat down.

It was clear that they meant serious business and that the map was the reason they were there. Marty, along with the others was marched from the Mess, objections or not, the map still in the hands of the Military Police.

From the guard-room the sergeant was taken to an inner room and interrogated. One by one the men were also interviewed, so that it took quite some time, in all.

William didn't want his father to go away without him. He felt that if he hadn't been a big boy of ten he might have cried. He was, in fact, allowed to go with Bill for the questioning. This, it turned out, was a strategic move rather than a kindness.

When they returned to the outer room, everyone was sombre. Marty's normal buoyancy had not only receded: it had plummeted. It became patently obvious that they were being treated as spies. He envisaged being taken down to the dungeons and locked in there forever.

It had been suggested to all of them that they were marking positions for the benefit of the enemy, even to the point that they had colluded with the sergeant and brought the boy as a cover. A double bluff. Not a new trick.

To Bill's mind the situation was becoming a farce. It might even have been a big laugh, if the position did not have really serious implications.

Although they offered the only explanation they could, it was hours before the two majors were summoned. There was no doubt about their irritation, nor was there any effort to muffle the raised voices beyond the wall where they had met the captors of the small party. In time they spared the men further embarrassment, secured their release and soon they were heading home along with the inoffensive map. The sergeant was in fact present for the discourse between the two officers and the Military Police and lived to tell the tale on many occasions after the war.

In the meantime pigeons flew and pigeons raced, as they still do. I can hear them as they fly in flocks over my house and when I do, I think of the boy who lived in a man's world, just for a day.

During the heyday of the Durham Coalfield in 1913 there were 304 pits with 165,246 miners working in them. Now none are left.

BLACK DEATH
Janet Evans

Me Dad was one and both me Grandads,
and there were uncles by the score.
But that was in days long, long past,
and now they are no more.
They had large white eyes and flashing teeth,
and lips so ruby red,
all shining out from ebony faces.
But now that race is dead.
Going in-by for eight hour shifts,
deep in the bowels of the earth,
they suffered clogged-up lungs and broken backs
to give a purpose to their birth.

Now the pits will be flooded,
no more hewing black diamonds from the seams.
A tradition crippled by greed and time,
leaving a million shattered dreams.
There will be no more fluttering banners,
no brass bands with beating drum.
There will be no more mates and marras,
the miner's life is over and done.

For the working man, off-course betting was not made legal until 1956.

AGAINST THE ODDS
Janet Evans

Standing on shaded street corners, bookie's runner by name,
watching with furtive glances, gambling the game.
Avoid the long arm of the law at all costs,
otherwise hard earned commission is lost.
Sixpence each way on a favoured nag, the usual bet,
written on grubby bits of paper, then the deal is set.
If fate has dealt a cruel blow, and writing can't be done,
word of mouth and basic trust let the illiterate have their fun.
Now and then it all goes wrong, and our runner is arrested.
Fines are paid by the big boys, the law's patience sorely tested.

Jazz bands are part of the culture in the North East. Nearly every family in our village had at least one member in the Jazz Band until it was disbanded. It is greatly missed.

THE JAZZ BAND OUTING
Tina O'Neill

Just like Christmas, it comes round every year, the Jazz Band trip to Blackpool.

With picnics, sun cream, sick bags and brollies we wait on street corners. Three coaches have been hired to take committee and children, with their parents in tow, for a day of sun, sand and sea.

With a bang, a clatter and a puff of smoke the buses arrive. They are not quite what we were expecting, but the drivers assure us they are perfectly safe. We climb aboard and the singing begins. 'We're all going on a summer holiday', soon turns into 'Singing in the rain', as the heavens open and rainwater starts coming up through the floor. Bags and feet are soon on seats, trying to stay dry. The bus in front still belches out thick, black smoke, and the one behind unloads all its adult passengers, just to get up the hill. They walk up, huddled under brollies. Slowly, but surely, the bus reaches the top, some ten minutes after the walkers. The kids think it's a great laugh, parents shout at the committee, who wonder why they even bother doing this, year after year.

When we pull into Blackpool, the sun begins to shine and it looks as though it could be a good day. As we pour from the buses, the drivers assure us all will be well for the return journey. We agree to be back at the buses by seven p.m. for a tour of the lights, before heading home.

The children spend the morning building sandcastles on the beach. The mothers walk miles around the shops and stop for the odd game of Bingo. Some lucky fathers manage to escape to the pub. Dinner is Fish and Chips, followed by candyfloss and toffee apples. The rest of the day is spent on the funfair. The kids want to see who can ride the biggest ride and still keep their lunch down, while mothers and fathers try their luck on the bandits.

We gather back at the buses with empty purses, tired and ready for home. After a head count we discover that we are missing one, so we wait. By eight o'clock, we are still one missing and a little worried. We decide to wait and to send the other two buses on their way. Two of the men go on a search.

We wait.

The kids are bored and begin to fight, the bus driver is moaning that he has other jobs to do.

We wait.

The wives of the two men on the search party are convinced that they have gone to the pub for a quick pint, and decide to go looking for them. Now we are missing five.

The children are laughing hysterically and women are rushing off the bus. It seems, the little darlings have bought live crabs for ten pence each, and they are running races up and down the aisle of the bus. We send the driver to collect the crabs with a bucket and spade.

As he steps from the bus with his captives, we hear the sound of approaching police cars. They screech to a halt in front of our bus, and our five missing passengers pile out. It appears they managed to report themselves missing at the same police station, after they all got lost. We thank the policemen by giving them the bucket of crabs and depart quickly, before they can return our gift. By the time we reach home, it is one a.m. and we promise ourselves, 'never again!'

Well, not until next year, at least.

≈ 21st Century ≈

It is impossible to predict the items which might appear in a 'Monks, Miners and Moonshine' of the third Millennium but the contributors of the following pieces could well have some influence on the first part of it.

The pupils of both Brandon Junior School and Hamsteels Primary School accepted the challenge to write stories based on interviewing their parents and grandparents. Valley Writers are indebted for the co-operation of the teachers in these schools on this part of the project.

Appreciation has to be expressed, also, to the impartiality of Pauline Walden, on whom the group dumped (no other word describes it) the unenviable task of selecting six entries from a list of almost forty. Selection was made even harder because of the varied ages of the children.

The presentation of their work, in particular, showed skill and imagination, varying from computer generated graphics to hand painted impressionism.

Unfortunately, the variety of original scripts presented too many technical problems to consider exact reproduction in this book. However, in transcribing them as exactly as possible, Valley Writers have attempted to retain and portray their original charm.

The group hopes that You, the reader, also finds them so.

AUNTY MARY AND UNCLE BOB
Toni Armstrong, 7 years

When My Mam was Little She Loved going to her aunty Marry' She Lived at the top of awer street. She Loved the Smell as She walked into her house. My uncle Bob used to fix watches and She Loved to sit and watch. I would Spend all day in Their house I loved Them very much.

MY NANA IRIS
Ryan Brown, 7 years

My Nana Iris is 75 years old. She lived at Cornsay when she was a little girl. That is where I live now. The house she lived in is not there now. She had 2 brother's and 2 sister's. They didn't have many toy's. She had a spinning top, and a hula hoop. One day her friend got a new bike and let my nana have a go. My nana was so pleased she rode very fast. Her friend shouted to her 'pull the brake!' but my nana was busy ringing the bell and the bike took my nana flying into a neighbour's hall way inside the house.

MY GRANDMA GRIMWOOD
Sarah Grimwood, 10 years

My Grandma Grimwood was born at bearpark on November the 12th, 1933. When she was two she moved to Ushaw Moor, at the bottom of the bank leading to Newbrancepeth, where her dad, who was a barber had his shop. My grandma's name is Cathrine, which is also her mothers name, and while they were living above the barbers her sister Josie was born. Half a mile away in Newbrancepeth my grandad Arthur Grimwood was born at about the same time but they were not to meet until 20 years later, because when my grandma was six (in 1939) when the second world began, the family moved away to Bradford in Yorkshire. All through the war, (which ended in 1945) my grandma remembers going to school wearing a bag containing her gas mask. All the children had them, and they all had to cope with air raids, blackouts and the fear of being bombed which we cannot imagine Nowadays. One of her friends was a girl called 'Billie Whitelaw' who later became a famous actress in the 1960s. Food had to be shared out in the war and somethings and like chocolate were very hard to get. My grandma remembers queing for over an hour for fruit when she was twelve and was finily givin some shriveled brown banana's, the first one's she had ever seen.

When she was ten they took in evacuees for the first time. The first children that came to them (a boy and a girl) they thought they were from a rough area. My grandma and her sister Josie thought that they were very funny because they wouldn't take a bath nor eat until my grandmother had tasted it first.

CHRISTMAS AT 7 ALBERT STREET IN THE YEAR 1935
Sian Cruise, 11 years

On Christmas Eve my grandas mother would make a new clippy mat for Christmas Day. While my granda and his twelve brothers and sisters would go to the cinema and pay two empty jam jars each as entrance fees. On Christmas Eve night my granda would share a bed with one of his brothers. It was so cold in the night that they wrapped a hot oven shelf in a blanket to keep warm because there was no heating.

On Christmas morning my granda would get a plain long sock which contained an apple an orange a few mixed nuts and three old pennies. There would also be visitors which would come for a Christmas drink. The dinner would be usually Turkey and Yorkshire puddings and for sweet there would be Christmas pudding. They had a real tree with baubles and a few cards. The salvation army band would come round the streets and play Christmas carols. When the day was nearly over my grandas mother would make butterfly cakes, trifle and scones for tea.

My granda always says to me it was a lovely Christmas when I was a boy.

MEMORIES
Daniel Thompson, 11 years

My Nana's Name Is Margaret She Was Born At Blaydon And Moved To Brandon And Went To Brandon School Then At 11Yrs Of Age Went On To Whinney Hill And New College. When She Came Home From School She Used To Play At A Place Called The Wreck. To Earn Some Pocket Money She Delivered Telegrams From Brandon Post Office. She Had To Go To Sunday School Every Week Which Was At St Johns Church Meadowfield. She Went Potatoe Picking For Charlie Harle At High Brandon; But Most Picking Was Done At The Fields In Browney Her Dad Used To Take Her Fishing To Whitby.

She Had Three Brothers And Played Along Lowland Road As In Those Days There Was No Shops Or Houses Built There. She Also Went Swimming At Durham Baths. In The Winter They All Had Sledges And Went Sledging After School. They Also Had A Coalfire And She Helped To Put The Logs In The Coalhouse Which Was Delivered To Their House. One Of Her Brothers Was Not Born Until My Nana Was 15Yrs Old So She Had To Help Her Mum Look After Him And Do Some Of The Chores. In Meadowfield There Was A Picture House Which Was Called The Hall. The Co Op Was The Council Officers And Had A Slaughter House At The Side And At The Other Side Was The Co Op Funeral Parlour Where They Made The Coffins.

CHILDHOOD MEMORIES
Brittony Brown, 9 years

This weekend I asked my grandparents about their childhood memories. My grandad told me his earliest childhood memory was not a very happy one! When he was 7 years old, he caught scarlet fever. His mum had to nurse him from home, and when he was nearly better his mum caught scarlet fever aswell! They were both taken to hospital and because my grandad was nearly better he had to stay in hospital with her. He had a fun time playing with games. He thought it was great fun!

Another strong memory was also what my grandad could remember it was when the 2nd world war broke out. It was 3rd Sept, 1939 and my grandad was 11 years old. He was listening to the news on the raidio because there was no television. His mum started to cry, and as he grew older he realised that his mum could remember the 1st world war and that nearly all of the family died, so it was just her and a few others who suvived and some of her friends died too.

Then my nanny said that one of her childhood memories was of going on holiday to Moreton, My nanny was about 8-9 years old. There they had very hot summers and while she was there she lived in a tent. Outside of the tent was a massive wooden slide. My nanny climbed up and slid down and because it was hot my nanny got a splinter in her bottom! Her daddy lay her across the bed and with a needle he tried to get it out. In the end he did but it was very sore.

Her second memory was like my grandad's, about the second world war. She had an air-raid shelter at the bottom of the garden and when there was an air-raid by the german planes, my nanny and her family went to the shelter to be safe from dropping bombs. These were called doodlebugs. The raids happened night after night so they just got used to it.

When nanny and grandad told me about the war, I realised how lucky I am to be living my childhood now with no bombs falling around me.

Acknowledgements

First of all, Valley Writers thank, most gratefully, Durham City Arts and the Arts Council of England, without whose generous assistance this Anthology would not have seen daylight.

The programme of research and tuition which followed from this, encouraged the imagination of group members to fly and, as a result we hope, dry and dusty history books have been turned into real people who had many of the same problems as we experience today. Local schoolchildren were encouraged to realise that what happened ten minutes ago is already history and were rewarded for discovering and revealing the memories of their Parents and Grandparents. Children were not the only beneficiaries, however, as everyone involved gained a greater awareness and knowledge of our Northern heritage.

Special thanks have to be said to those tutors who risked their sanity by laying out their knowledge and expertise to be freely picked over. In datal order of their ordeal, they were Pauline Walden, David Simpson, Norman Emery, Kitty Fitzgerald, Michael Standen, Gillian Allnutt, Kathleen McCreery and Fiona Cooper. Appreciation should also be recorded for the assistance of the staff at the museums of Beamish, Hartlepool, South Shields, Bowes and Sunderland; the libraries of Durham, South Shields, Shildon and Sunderland and for the facilities afforded to us at Ushaw College.

Closer to home; Anne Chalder and Alison Atyeo of Esh Winning Library, will no doubt be delighted that they can return to routine duties, now that the Valley Writers project is ended.

Once again, the bulk of the responsibility for the final product fell on the capable shoulders of Margaret Lewis. Her expertise is invaluable, her encouragement irreplaceable and her reliability abused shamelessly.

BOOKS USED AS SOURCE MATERIAL

G.W.O. Addleshaw, *Blanchland, A Short History*

Correlli Barnett, *World War I, The Story of the Great War 1914 - 1918*

J. Burke, *Buffalo Bill*

J.C. Cannell, *The Secrets of Houdini*

Timothy Eden, *Durham, Volumes 1 and 2*

William Fordyce, *The History and Antiquities of the County Palatine of Durham, Volume 1*

Frank Graham, *Famous Northern Battles*

M.H. Hayes, *Stable Management*

John McCutcheon, *Troubled Seams*

Arthur Mee, *The King's England: Durham*

Edwin Miller, *Eyewitness*

Philip Nixon and Denis Dunlop, *Exploring Durham History*

Paul Perry and Derek Dodds, *Curiosities of County Durham*

Tom Pickard, *The Jarrow March*

D. Pocock and R. Norris, *A History of County Durham*

Richardson, Durham, *Cathedral City*

David Simpson, *Durham Millennium*

John Sykes, *Local Records or Historical Records of Northumberland and Durham, Newcastle upon Tyne and Berwick upon Tweed, Volumes I and II*

*Back Row: Ron Gray, Tina O'Neill, David Cummings,
Janet Evans, John Gamblin, Clive Conway
Front Row: Sandra Salmon, Betty Bone, Alice Smith, Eve Stockmann*

Valley Writers, as the picture shows, is a group of mixed age and experience but with a purpose in common. That is: to write to the best of one's ability, to have fun doing so and to encourage others to do the same by showing that writing is not an elitist pastime. The group meets on most Friday afternoons in Esh Winning Library and gives a welcome to anyone wishing to join them.

'Monks, Miners and Moonshine' is the second collection of work by Valley Writers which has received support from Durham City Arts and the Arts Council of England, for which the group is immensely grateful. To those who were kind enough (or should that be brave enough?) to read 'Write Up Your Valley', our first offering, we say thank you and hope that evolving skills will make this selection even more enjoyable.